THE WONDER OF WALKING BY FAITH

Retreat Leader Guide
WORKBOOK
RICHARD T. CASE

*To my wife, Linda, who has an amazing heart of Faith —
to have us hear what God authors (speaks to us)
and then patiently receive His gift of faith
as He perfects or finishes faith in us.
We have seen and continue to experience
mighty and wonderful works of God in our lives —
only things that He can do; and Linda knows that without faith
it is impossible to please God so she does not let us try
to figure things out on our own—she says:
"Why bother —we are called to walk by faith,
and there is no other way to walk." She will not let us
give up or get discouraged when things are delayed
or not quite happening like we were expecting—
just stay with the process of faith: Faith comes from hearing
and hearing from the Word. I am so blessed
that we have learned this important truth together
and that I have a spouse who lives this out as a way of life.
What a privilege.*

Acknowledgments

We wish to thank all of the leaders of our **Ministry: Living Waters—ABIDE Ministries!** These leaders are also learning how to live in faith and bear witness to the wonder of God's faithfulness to His supernatural work in their lives—and together we are giving this away to others who are learning how critical it is to live by faith. Thank you all:

These leaders are:

Jake & Mary Beckel
Joe & Leigh Bogar
Rich & Janet Cocchiaro
Larry & Sherry Collet
David & Melissa Dunkel
Tom & Susanne Ewing
Rick & Kelly Ferris
Joel & Christina Gunn
Scott & Terry Hitchcock
Chris & Jaclyn Hoover
Rick & Nancy Hoover
Tad & Monica Jones
Ed & Becky Kobel
Don & Rachelle Light
Chris & Heidi May
Terry & Josephine Noetzel
Steve & Carolyn Van Ooteghem
Preston & Lynda Pitts
Dan & Kathy Rocconi
Bob & Keri Rockwell
John & Michelle Santaferraro
Allyson & Denny Weinberg
Neal & Kathy Weisenburger

THE WONDERS OF WALKING BY FAITH
PUBLISHED BY LIVING WATERS—ABIDE MINISTRIES
7615 Lemon Gulch Way
Castle Rock, CO 80108

Unless otherwise noted, all Scripture quotations are from the ESV® Bible (The Holy Bible, English Standard Version®), copyright © 2001 by Crossway Bibles, a publishing ministry of Good News Publishers. Used by permission. All rights reserved.

ISBN: 978-1-7334151-7-0

Copyright © 2024 by Richard T. Case.

All rights reserved. No part of this publication may be reproduced, distributed or transmitted in any form or by any means, including photocopying, recording, or other electronic or mechanical methods, without the prior written permission of the publisher.

Publisher's Cataloging-in-Publication data

Names:
Title:
Description: .
Identifiers: ISBN | LCCN
Subjects:

Printed in the United States of America 2024 — 2nd ed

TABLE OF CONTENTS

Lesson One:
Introduction. 2

Lesson Two:
Why is Faith Necessary?. 22

Lesson Three:
Why Is It so Easy to Live Without Faith, in Unbelief?. 32

Lesson Four:
What Are the Results of Unbelief?. 46

Lesson Five:
How Do We Operate in Faith?. 54

Lesson Six:
How Do We Operate in Faith? (Continued) .64

Lesson Seven:
What Are the Results of Faith? (Continued). 82

Lesson Eight:
Examples. 92

LESSON 1:
INTRODUCTION:

Read Hebrews 10:35-39:

35 Therefore do not throw away your confidence, which has a great reward. 36 For you have need of endurance, so that when you have done the will of God you may receive what is promised. 37 For,

"Yet a little while,
 and the coming one will come and will not delay;
38 but my righteous one shall live by faith,
 and if he shrinks back,
my soul has no pleasure in him."

39 But we are not of those who shrink back and are destroyed, but of those who have faith and preserve their souls.

We are called as followers of Christ to walk by faith! The Lord states clearly that He has no pleasure in us if we walk by sight—rather, all of His children are called to walk by faith. This course, then, is intended to teach us what faith actually is and how we walk in that faith to live as God intended.

Word Meanings:

Just: used of him whose way of thinking, feeling, and acting is wholly conformed to the will of God, and who, therefore, needs no rectification in the heart or life
Live: to enjoy real life; to have true life and worthy of the name; active, blessed, endless in the kingdom of God; to live (i.e., pass life) in the manner of the living and acting
Faith: to be persuaded, to allow one's self to be persuaded; to be induced to believe: to have complete confidence in a thing

LESSON 1:
INTRODUCTION:

CURRENT EVALUATION OF MY LIFE OF FAITH:

What is the truth about your current walk of faith? Rate the following from 1 to 5 (1 being best and couldn't be better, 5 being worst):

1. Hearing from God regularly and receiving His Word for me: 1 2 3 4 5

2. Am responding to how God is challenging me with greater opportunities to believe His ways, His purposes, His work in my life: 1 2 3 4 5

3. Understand with clarity the promises of God to me: 1 2 3 4 5

4. Seeing that is it is becoming easier for me to believe these promises: 1 2 3 4 5

5. Regularly experience God's great and mighty works as I respond in faith to His promises to me: 1 2 3 4 5

6. I am not trying to have more faith—but instead receive what He has for me: 1 2 3 4 5

7. I fully understand how to grow in a life of faith: 1 2 3 4 5

1. FAITH DEFINED

Read and write out the following verses. With regard to the essence of faith, who do these verses say is the object of our faith?

> - **John 1:6-14:**
>
> [6] There was a man sent from God, whose name was John. [7] He came as a witness, to bear witness about the light, that all might believe through him. [8] He was not the light but came to bear witness about the light.
>
> [9] The true light, which gives light to everyone, was coming into the world. [10] He was in the world, and the world was made through him, yet the world did not

LESSON 1:
INTRODUCTION:

> know him. ¹¹ He came to his own,[a] and his own people[b] did not receive him. ¹² But to all who did receive him, who believed in his name, he gave the right to become children of God, ¹³ who were born, not of blood nor of the will of the flesh nor of the will of man, but of God.
>
> ¹⁴ And the Word became flesh and dwelt among us, and we have seen his glory, glory as of the only Son[c] from the Father, full of grace and truth.

_____
_____
_____
_____
_____

   Jesus is the Word. He is God. He is the light. He is the creator of all and is the object of our faith, in whom we are to believe—in Him and in all that He does and says. He has the Power and Life to give us; and all emanates from Him—and to those who receive Him, He gives this ability to believe (have faith).

Word Meanings:

Light: God is light because light has the extremely delicate, subtle, pure, brilliant quality of truth and its knowledge, together with the spiritual purity associated with it

Receive: to take with the hand, lay hold of, any person or thing in order to use it; to take up a thing to be carried; to take upon one's self; to take in order to carry away

Power: the power of authority (influence) and of right (privilege); the power of rule or government (the power of him whose will and commands must be submitted to by others and obeyed)

Sons of God (children of God): in the Old Testament, they are "the people of Israel" as especially dear to God; in the New Testament, in Paul's writings, they are all who are led by the Spirit of God and thus closely related to God

Believe: to think to be true, to be persuaded of, to credit, place confidence in of the thing believed

Name: the name is used for everything that the name covers, everything the thought or feeling of which is aroused in the mind by mentioning, hearing, remembering, the name, (i.e. for one's rank, authority, interests, pleasure, command, excellences, deeds, etc.)

LESSON 1:
INTRODUCTION:

> - **John 6:29:**
>
> ²⁹ Jesus answered them, "This is the work of God, that you believe in him whom he has sent."

_____
_____
_____
_____
_____

    Most believers think that the work of a Christian is to do things for God. However, the real work, as Christ states, is to believe, to have faith in what He will speak to us. This lines up with the introductory statement that the just shall walk by faith, which is our real work; not doing things for Him but believing by walking in faith.

Word Meanings: **Work:** business, employment, that which any one is occupied; that which one undertakes to do, enterprise, undertaking
Believe: to think to be true, to be persuaded of, to credit, place confidence in of the thing believed

> - **John 11:17-27:**
>
> I Am the Resurrection and the Life
> ¹⁷ Now when Jesus came, he found that Lazarus had already been in the tomb four days. ¹⁸ Bethany was near Jerusalem, about two miles[a] off, ¹⁹ and many of the Jews had come to Martha and Mary to console them concerning their brother. ²⁰ So when Martha heard that Jesus was coming, she went and met him, but Mary remained seated in the house. ²¹ Martha said to Jesus, "Lord, if you had been here, my brother would not have died. ²² But even now I know that whatever you ask from God, God will give you." ²³ Jesus said to her, "Your brother will rise again." ²⁴ Martha said to him, "I know that he will rise again in the resurrection on the last day." ²⁵ Jesus said to her, "I am the

LESSON 1:
INTRODUCTION:

> resurrection and the life.[b] Whoever believes in me, though he die, yet shall he live, 26 and everyone who lives and believes in me shall never die. Do you believe this?" 27 She said to him, "Yes, Lord; I believe that you are the Christ, the Son of God, who is coming into the world."

_____
_____
_____
_____
_____

As Jesus explained to Martha, the real walk of faith is in believing that the power and our life rest in the power and life of the resurrection of Jesus. Not only is He talking about eternal life but also the power of the present life of walking in faith by following Jesus, who is living in His life of the Resurrection, no longer an Earthly life that He demonstrated prior to His death and resurrection, but nor in the fullness of all the powers of God. He now had supernatural power that is above all things material, including our circumstances and situations. As He asked Martha: Do you believe this?

Word Meanings:

Life: of the absolute fullness of life, both essential and ethical, which belongs to God, and through Him both to the hypostatic "logos" and to Christ in whom the "logos" put on human nature, life real and genuine, a life active and vigorous, devoted to God, blessed, in the portion even in this world of those who put their trust in Christ, but after the resurrection to be consummated by new accessions (among them a more perfect body), and to last forever

Believe: to think to be true, to be persuaded of, to credit, place confidence in of the thing believed

Christ "anointed": Christ was the Messiah, the Son of God

- **Hebrews 11:6:**

  6 And without faith it is impossible to please him, for whoever would draw near to God must believe that he exists and that he rewards those who seek him.

LESSON 1:
INTRODUCTION:

_____
_____
_____
_____
_____

This lays out an important truth that without faith it's impossible to please God. Think about the two-fold significance of that:

1. We will not be able to create a life of pure comfort or safety where we protect ourselves from ever having to be challenged by the troubles/tribulations of the world.

2. We will not be blessed by new adventures that come when we walk by faith in what God is doing in our lives. Why? Because without faith, it is impossible to please God.

As He demonstrates His wonderful love and care for us, He offers us a means to walk with Him in a way that actually is not difficult, but first we must believe that He is the "I am" (note: in English this translates as "He is") and that He is able to handle and provide solutions to anything we encounter and need because He is Almighty God. We have to fully receive in our mind that He is a rewarder to those who diligently seek Him. What is the reward? Think of what we need to please Him: faith. That is the reward. He will give us the faith we need (which is what this course is going to teach us) to diligently seek Him (to stay with Him until He gives us the faith). This is a beautiful gift: He does not make it impossible for us to be faithful. Instead, He offers a way to faith Himself so that we can meet His condition. This is the very reason this course is so important: to learn how to receive God's gift.

Word Meanings:

Believe: to think to be true, to be persuaded of, to credit, place confidence in of the thing believed

I AM: Name of God to mean everything there is, everything we need – God Almighty

LESSON 1:
INTRODUCTION:

Read through these verses and define "What" is faith:

> - **Hebrews 11:1-3:**
>
> By Faith
> **11** Now faith is the assurance of things hoped for, the conviction of things not seen. ² For by it the people of old received their commendation. ³ By faith we understand that the universe was created by the word of God, so that what is seen was not made out of things that are visible.

_____
_____
_____
_____
_____

First, in verse three, the Scripture states that the world was created by what God spoke. So, the material and all of creation is subordinated or subject to the power of what God speaks. This means that your circumstances, since we operate in the natural, are subject to what God can fulfill through what He speaks, and thus, because the spiritual trumps all that is material, it can resolve, solve, and change supernaturally. As we previously learned, then, He is the "I am," and nothing is too difficult for Him.

This is why He defines faith as the substance (something real) of things hoped for you (expected) and the evidence (certainty) of things not seen. As you ponder what is certain of things not seen (what will happen for sure that has not happened yet), we only have one answer—what God speaks! God is trustworthy and because what He speaks supersedes our circumstances, He defines faith as believing with certainty (absolutely no doubt) that what He has said will happen, even though it has not happened yet.

The two elements of faith will be:
   1. Do we have clarity about what He speaks?
   2. Do we believe with certainty what He has spoken?

As we go through this course, we will learn the depth and practical ways of learning these two elements.

LESSON 1:
INTRODUCTION:

Word Meanings: **Faith:** to be persuaded, to allow one's self to be persuaded; to be induced to
believe: to have complete confidence in a thing
Substance: that which has foundation, is firm that which has actual existence; a substance, real being—title deed, ownership
Hope: expectation of good, joy
Assurance/Conviction: a proof, that by which a thing is proved or tested, certainty; things that which have been done, a deed, an accomplished fact; what is done or being accomplished
Not Seen: to perceive by the senses, to feel; to discover by use, to know by experience
Good Report: to be a witness, to bear witness, (i.e., to affirm that one has seen or heard or experienced something, or that he knows it because taught by the divine)
Framed: complete; to fit out, equip, put in order, arrange, adjust
Word of God: Rhema
Not Visible: to become evident, to be brought forth into the light, come to view

2. WHY IS IT NECESSARY TO LIVE BY FAITH?

Let's review the real spiritual necessity for why we are called to live by faith. Read through these verses in Genesis and write down how the world was created; the authority that was given to Adam and Eve, and the harmony between the spiritual and the physical (as was through the spiritual: God's spoken Word).

- **Genesis 1:26-31; Genesis 2:8-25: The Garden of Eden:**

26 Then God said, "Let us make man[a] in our image, after our likeness. And let them have dominion over the fish of the sea and over the birds of the heavens and over the livestock and over all the earth and over every creeping thing that creeps on the earth."

27 So God created man in his own image,
  in the image of God he created him;
  male and female he created them.

28 And God blessed them. And God said to them, "Be fruitful and multiply and fill the earth and subdue it, and have dominion over the fish of the sea and over the birds of the heavens and over every living thing that moves on the earth." 29 And God said, "Behold, I have given you every plant yielding seed that is on the face of all the earth, and every tree with seed in its fruit. You shall have

LESSON 1:
INTRODUCTION:

them for food. ³⁰ And to every beast of the earth and to every bird of the heavens and to everything that creeps on the earth, everything that has the breath of life, I have given every green plant for food." And it was so. ³¹ And God saw everything that he had made, and behold, it was very good. And there was evening and there was morning, the sixth day.

⁸ And the Lord God planted a garden in Eden, in the east, and there he put the man whom he had formed. ⁹ And out of the ground the Lord God made to spring up every tree that is pleasant to the sight and good for food. The tree of life was in the midst of the garden, and the tree of the knowledge of good and evil.
¹⁰ A river flowed out of Eden to water the garden, and there it divided and became four rivers. ¹¹ The name of the first is the Pishon. It is the one that flowed around the whole land of Havilah, where there is gold. ¹² And the gold of that land is good; bdellium and onyx stone are there. ¹³ The name of the second river is the Gihon. It is the one that flowed around the whole land of Cush. ¹⁴ And the name of the third river is the Tigris, which flows east of Assyria. And the fourth river is the Euphrates.

¹⁵ The Lord God took the man and put him in the garden of Eden to work it and keep it. ¹⁶ And the Lord God commanded the man, saying, "You may surely eat of every tree of the garden, ¹⁷ but of the tree of the knowledge of good and evil you shall not eat, for in the day that you eat[a] of it you shall surely die."

¹⁸ Then the Lord God said, "It is not good that the man should be alone; I will make him a helper fit for[b] him." ¹⁹ Now out of the ground the Lord God had formed[c] every beast of the field and every bird of the heavens and brought them to the man to see what he would call them. And whatever the man called every living creature, that was its name. ²⁰ The man gave names to all livestock and to the birds of the heavens and to every beast of the field. But for Adam[d] there was not found a helper fit for him. ²¹ So the Lord God caused a deep sleep to fall upon the man, and while he slept took one of his ribs and closed up its place with flesh. ²² And the rib that the Lord God had taken from the man he made[e] into a woman and brought her to the man. ²³ Then the man said,

"This at last is bone of my bones
    and flesh of my flesh;
she shall be called Woman,
    because she was taken out of Man."[f]

LESSON 1:
INTRODUCTION:

> ²⁴ Therefore a man shall leave his father and his mother and hold fast to his wife, and they shall become one flesh. ²⁵ And the man and his wife were both naked and were not ashamed.

_____
_____
_____
_____
_____

As we have discussed in other studies, God created, by speaking into existence, a perfect world, where the spiritual and the physical were in perfect harmony with each other. This harmony had seven characteristics whereby God's intended life for man and woman before the fall was exceptional:

1. Exceptional Authority
2. Exceptional Provision
3. Exceptional Identity
4. Exceptional Work
5. Exceptional Marriage
6. Exceptional Health and Healing
7. Exceptional Communion with God

This did not require faith, as everything was operating in sync together. The spiritual and physical were in harmony, and so what was seen and experienced was both spiritual and physical at the same time. Adam and Eve were in perfect communion with the triune God. There was no "sin nature"—no destruction, no work of the enemy, as everything was in a complete state of perfection and harmony, so there was no call for "faith." All was instantly believed and received—there was no reason for any thought of doubt or not receiving.

Word Meanings:

Make: fashion, accomplish
Dominion: Splendor, majesty, beauty, vigor, glory; in charge, control, have jurisdiction, power to influence; cause to become: great; much; many; enlarged, exceedingly abundant; Power (physical and spiritual) of doing supernatural; right to govern, rule, command—possessing authority; mighty work, strength, miracle; performing miracles; excellence

LESSON 1:
INTRODUCTION:

Made: same word as make, fashion, accomplish
Very: exceedingly, abundant
Good: pleasant, agreeable (to the senses); pleasant (to the higher nature), excellent, rich, valuable in estimation: glad, happy, prosperous
Leave: forsake, to depart from, leave behind, let alone, abandon, to let loose, set free, let go, free
Cleave: stay close, keep close, stick to, stick with, follow closely, join to, to stay with, to be joined together
One: unity, agreement, only, once, once for all

Now, read through these verses to fully understand how the physical was created and is subordinated, subject to the spiritual, God speaking:

> - **Genesis 1:1-2; 1:31:**
>
> The Creation of the World
> **1** In the beginning, God created the heavens and the earth. [2] The earth was without form and void, and darkness was over the face of the deep. And the Spirit of God was hovering over the face of the waters.
>
> [31] And God saw everything that he had made, and behold, it was very good. And there was evening and there was morning, the sixth day.

_____
_____
_____
_____
_____

Word Meanings: **Created:** birthed, of something new; miraculous
Said: Hebrew word, same as Rhema

LESSON 1:
INTRODUCTION:

> - **Colossians 1:15-18:**
>
> The Preeminence of Christ
> [15] He is the image of the invisible God, the firstborn of all creation. [16] For by[a] him all things were created in heaven and on earth, visible and invisible, whether thrones or dominions or rulers or authorities—all things were created through him and for him. [17] And he is before all things, and in him all things hold together. [18] And he is the head of the body, the church. He is the beginning, the firstborn from the dead, that in everything he might be preeminent.

_____
_____
_____
_____
_____

God said…And it was so; It is important to understand as we set the foundations for faith that God spoke the material into existence by speaking, and that all was created by, for, in, and with the power of Christ. He and the spoken Word are superior to the material (and your circumstances), have the power over the material (and your circumstances), and that nothing is greater than this power. He and His creative power are preeminent. As we learn of living by faith, it is critical that we understand this important truth.

Word Meanings:

Image: Christ on account of His divine nature; invisible: unseen, or that which cannot be seen
Things: all things, everything
Created: to form, shape, (i.e., to completely change or transform)
Heavens: the region above the sidereal heavens, the seat of order of things eternal and consummately perfect where God dwells with other heavenly beings
Earth: the abode of men and animals; a country, land enclosed within fixed boundaries, a tract of land, territory, region
Visible: to see with the eyes; to see with the mind, to perceive, know; to see, i.e. become acquainted with by experience, to experience
Invisible: unseen, or that which cannot be seen
Thrones: kingly power or royalty
Dominion: power, lordship, government

LESSON 1:
INTRODUCTION:

Principalities: the first place, principality, rule, magistracy of angels and demons
Powers: the leading and more powerful among created beings superior to man, spiritual potentates
Consist: to put together, unite parts into one whole
Preeminence: first in rank; influence, honor

At the fall, mankind and the world experienced the death of the spiritual and now were controlled by Satan in the natural, physical world. Read through these verses and write what happened at the fall:

> - **Genesis 3:1-7:**
> The Fall
> **3** Now the serpent was more crafty than any other beast of the field that the Lord God had made.
>
> He said to the woman, "Did God actually say, 'You[a] shall not eat of any tree in the garden'?"² And the woman said to the serpent, "We may eat of the fruit of the trees in the garden, ³ but God said, 'You shall not eat of the fruit of the tree that is in the midst of the garden, neither shall you touch it, lest you die.'" ⁴ But the serpent said to the woman, "You will not surely die.⁵ For God knows that when you eat of it your eyes will be opened, and you will be like God, knowing good and evil." ⁶ So when the woman saw that the tree was good for food, and that it was a delight to the eyes, and that the tree was to be desired to make one wise,[b] she took of its fruit and ate, and she also gave some to her husband who was with her, and he ate.⁷ Then the eyes of both were opened, and they knew that they were naked. And they sewed fig leaves together and made themselves loincloths.

_____
_____
_____
_____
_____

Word Meanings: **Die:** kill, put to death

LESSON 1:
INTRODUCTION:

How did this happen (the enemy chose to rebel wishing to reign himself)?

> - **Isaiah 14:12-13:**
>
> [12] How you are fallen from heaven,
>   O Day Star, son of Dawn!
> How you are cut down to the ground,
>   you who laid the nations low!
> [13] You said in your heart,
>   I will ascend to heaven;
> above the stars of God
>   I will set my throne on high;
> I will sit on the mount of assembly
>   in the far reaches of the north…[a]

_____
_____
_____
_____
_____

The exceptional living given to Adam and Eve in the Garden of Eden was offered by God and was His original plan for all of mankind. Not only were they given authority over all the Earth, but they also were asked to be fruitful and multiply so that all the Earth beyond the original Garden of Eden would provide the perfect place for all of mankind to experience the exceptional living (the exceptional characteristics described in Session 2) planned by God. However, Satan came to the Garden of Eden and tempted Adam and Eve, according to the test of the free will (using the Tree of the Knowledge of Good and Evil).

There is a lot to consider when discussing man's fall in the Garden. First, where did Satan come from? We know he was a fallen angel. Originally named Lucifer, he was an angel of light who was one of the original created angels and part of the host who enjoyed life with God in heaven. He was a leader in heaven and had great stature. But as an angel created by God, we must note that Satan is not God and does not possess the qualities of God. This is one of the myths for most believers: that Satan and God tend to be somehow equivalent in power and scope, especially

LESSON 1:
INTRODUCTION:

in today's world. Satan is not omnipresent, omniscient, or omnipotent. Rather, he is finite and only has the characteristics and the powers of a spiritual created being.

As a leader in heaven, and also having a free will, Lucifer decided to attempt to become equal to God and achieve dominance in heaven. Of course, not being God, he had no power to achieve his overthrow bid and was cast out of heaven. Since all the angels had free will, God turned to them all to ask who they wished to follow. God or Lucifer? We know that one-third followed Satan (Revelation 12:4) and are now operating with Satan in what is called the spiritual realm as demons. Thus, two-thirds remained with God in heaven and are now operating in the spiritual realm as angels. In Revelation 5:11, it says that 10,000 x 10,000 are now worshiping God, so that number would equal 100,000,000 if taken literally. So, whether it is literal or just representing a massive number of angels, the good news is that there are twice as many angels as demons; and that an angel's purpose in our lives is to minister to us. (Hebrews 2:14)

Satan, then, taking the form of a serpent, appeals to Adam and Eve in the Garden of Eden to bring about this test of free will.

When Adam and Eve fell, they did so by making the pure mistake of not using their privilege of access and communion with God. Instead of asking Him to reiterate His instruction about the tree and the consequence of eating from it (since they were being confused by Satan), they exercised their free will— their self-will (the flesh)—and "died." What died? Their spiritual connectivity to God was destroyed so they were no longer "pure" or in a state of perfection necessary to continue their spiritual and holy relationship with God. Their nature changed, and thus, the nature of every offspring of Adam and Eve changed. All of mankind since, because of this sin of nature, has been separated from God and all stand condemned because of this separation by nature (John 3:18). They still were functioning humans with a body and soul but now could only enter eternity with God if they accepted a remedy to restore what had died.

The remedy to re-establish a relationship with God because of this nature is perfection. God's holy nature required perfection for such relationship. Since no one with this sinful, fallen nature could reach perfection, only God Himself could offer a remedy—to take the penalty required to establish a way for us to have relationship through believing what He did at the cross and then being resurrected for us. When we believe and receive Christ, we are "born again." His Holy Spirit enters us and makes us again alive, thus, returning us to the spiritual place that died when Adam and Eve exercised their free will and "sinned."

The world went from perfection to a state of kill, steal, and destroy under the dominion of the enemy—a permanent state of entropy—everything going to destruction.

LESSON 1:
INTRODUCTION:

> - **Luke 4:5-8:**
>
> ⁵ And the devil took him up and showed him all the kingdoms of the world in a moment of time, ⁶ and said to him, "To you I will give all this authority and their glory, for it has been delivered to me, and I give it to whom I will. ⁷ If you, then, will worship me, it will all be yours." ⁸ And Jesus answered him, "It is written,
>
> "'You shall worship the Lord your God,
> and him only shall you serve.'"

_____
_____
_____
_____
_____

Word Meanings: **Kingdom:** royal power, kingship, dominion, rule, not to be confused with an actual kingdom but rather the right or authority to rule over a kingdom
Power: same as authority, dominion
Give: deliver, grant to, hand over
Delivered: to give into the hands (of another); to give over into (one's) power or use; to deliver to one something to keep, use, take care of, manage

> - **1 John 5:18-20:**
>
> ¹⁸ We know that everyone who has been born of God does not keep on sinning, but he who was born of God protects him, and the evil one does not touch him. ¹⁹ We know that we are from God, and the whole world lies in the power of the evil one.
>
> ²⁰ And we know that the Son of God has come and has given us understanding, so that we may know him who is true; and we are in him who is true, in his Son Jesus Christ. He is the true God and eternal life.

LESSON 1:
INTRODUCTION:

_____
_____
_____
_____
_____

World: the circle of the Earth, the Earth; the inhabitants of the Earth, men, the human family

Control of Wickedness: full of labors, annoyances, hardships, pressed and harassed by labors, bringing toils, annoyances, perils; of a time full of peril to Christian faith and steadfastness; causing pain and trouble, bad, of a bad nature or condition, in a physical sense: diseased or blind; in an ethical sense: evil, wicked, bad

Here we see a world of destruction, decay:

> - **John 10:10:**
>
>   ¹⁰ The thief comes only to steal and kill and destroy.

_____
_____
_____
_____
_____

This force that now operates in our world under the nature of the enemy is called "entropy"—where everything left alone is moving toward destruction. We are living in a world that is characterized by steal, kill, and destroy. This destruction is the very nature of the enemy, a consequence of the fall in the Garden. With entropy, everything declines into disorder, falls apart, or is destroyed. This applies to physical things (even steel and iron bridges), organizations, governments, businesses, relationships, and marriages. (According to Christianity Today, February 14, 2014, currently 30 percent of all marriages—Christian and non-Christian alike—in the U.S. wind up in divorce.) Many more Christian marriages are in a state of separation and many families are in a state of dysfunctional dynamics.

LESSON 1:
INTRODUCTION:

Everything around us is moving toward not working and becoming more difficult. This is ironic in that technology is supposedly exploding to make things easier for us, but that, too, is because of steal, kill, and destroy (anyone heard of hacking and viruses),which also is contributing to destruction and falling apart. We live in a world of entropy, and none of us can escape it, which is why Paul says we are not just dealing with flesh and blood but powers and principalities.

How does the enemy use his demons to impact your life and personal world?

_____

_____

_____

Remember, the enemy is finite and is not omniscient, omnipotent, nor omnipresent. So, how does he and the demonic work? Satan's system operates in a hierarchy. The demonic at your personal level is particularly interested in thwarting God's will in your life by having you exercise your self-will and not follow God's will (same as with Adam and Eve). They do this through wiles or schemes (Ephesians 6:11). They are developing these strategies by observing you and your life. Because of our sinful nature, we already are geared toward making poor choices, living in the self, being away from God and His will for our lives, and being easily drawn to sin and the nature of the world. Our propensity is to follow our selfish desires, and thus, we are enticed to the things of the world that lead to destruction and the consequences of sin. Further, as we follow our selfish, sinful behavior, the enemy notices cause and effect (i.e., which things cause you to avoid spending time with God; which things get you angry; which things lead you to worry or be anxious; which things bring you fear; who you choose not to forgive; what causes you to overreact; what drives you to look at pornography or to drink, etc.).

As these demons observe these cause and effect relationships, they work to create more of the causes so that the effects get deeper and more often—developing what are called patterns, or what psychologists call wounds. Interestingly, the harder you try to overcome these patterns and wounds on your own (self-will), the more you fail, and the deeper they get. Eventually, you resign yourself to these behaviors, and the enemy takes you farther into other areas of new patterns, like guilt and failure. This is all out of his nature of steal, kill, and destroy—creating a world of entropy and a work of thwarting your life.

Word Meanings:

Thief: abuse their confidence for their own gain
Steal: take away by theft, (i.e., take away by stealth)
Destroy: to put out of the way entirely, abolish, put an end to, ruin, render useless

LESSON 1:
INTRODUCTION:

Now, when we fully understand all this, we see that "the spiritual" was separated from "the physical." No longer was God's perfect world in harmony, with everything working together. His sinless created beings were no longer walking in perfect harmony with Him in this perfect place. Rather His created beings had disobeyed and "died"—meaning they lost their spiritual connectivity with Him and were "condemned" to separation from Him. They did not yet have the remedy that would later be offered through Christ's redemptive work; so now there was no longer an ability for this harmony to operate naturally. Because of this separation, and because of our fallen nature (and also because we were being born again with the Holy Spirit residing within us), we can restore things in our lives by "walking by faith"—believing that what He speaks in the spiritual will bring together His work to the material (our circumstances). We will see how this all works in subsequent sessions.

LESSON 2:
WHY IS FAITH NECESSARY?

God created the heavens and the Earth by Him speaking—the Word created everything, so that the world, the natural (the material) we live in was and is subordinate to the spiritual. When first created, it was in a state of perfection, and Adam and Eve lived in a place of exceptional living that was intended for us all:

1. Exceptional Authority
2. Exceptional Provision
3. Exceptional Identity
4. Exceptional Work
5. Exceptional Marriage
6. Exceptional Health and Healing
7. Exceptional Communion with God

The only condition to their living this way (both them and their offspring/us) was that they follow one rule: do not eat from the Tree of the Knowledge of Good and Evil. Having the profound characteristic of free will in the image of God, they were tempted by the enemy and did exercise their free will in opposition to the instruction of the Father. This decision brought about the "fall." They handed to Satan the authority over the Earth and introduced entropy (a natural world of destruction and decay). At that moment their nature changed to one of self-centeredness, which we call the sin nature, a nature whereby we are spiritually separated from God and in need of a remedy to be restored to a life with God.

At the fall, the spiritual was separated from the physical. The two were no longer in harmony; and the physical was operating in a state of decay and ruin. It needed a remedy.

> "At the fall, the spiritual was separated from the physical. The two were no longer in harmony; and the physical was operating in a state of decay and ruin."

GOD PROVIDES A REMEDY:

Because of God's love and very nature, He Himself provided a remedy to this problem of separation of mankind who was now living in a fallen, destructive world.

Christ's death and resurrection restored authority and ushered in the Kingdom of God. This means that once again the spiritual can be supreme to the physical and work hand in hand (re-create Eden in our lives). Read through these verses and write down what they say about the process of providing a remedy for the fallen state of mankind and the world.

LESSON 2:
WHY IS FAITH NECESSARY?

> - **John 3:1-8:**
>
> You Must Be Born Again
> **3** Now there was a man of the Pharisees named Nicodemus, a ruler of the Jews. ² This man came to Jesus[a] by night and said to him, "Rabbi, we know that you are a teacher come from God, for no one can do these signs that you do unless God is with him." ³ Jesus answered him, "Truly, truly, I say to you, unless one is born again[b] he cannot see the kingdom of God." ⁴ Nicodemus said to him, "How can a man be born when he is old? Can he enter a second time into his mother's womb and be born?" ⁵ Jesus answered, "Truly, truly, I say to you, unless one is born of water and the Spirit, he cannot enter the kingdom of God. ⁶ That which is born of the flesh is flesh, and that which is born of the Spirit is spirit.[c] ⁷ Do not marvel that I said to you, 'You[d] must be born again.' ⁸ The wind[e] blows where it wishes, and you hear its sound, but you do not know where it comes from or where it goes. So it is with everyone who is born of the Spirit."

_____
_____
_____
_____
_____

Given that we live in a world of entropy, characterized by kill, steal, and destroy; and every person born into the world stands condemned because of their separation from God, the world and each person are in need of a remedy. Christ's death on the cross and resurrection provided that remedy. He related to Nicodemus that we "must be born again," which comes when we express our belief of what Christ completed at the cross and through His resurrection. Upon that expression of belief, the Spirit then re-enters your inner soul, your inner life, and begins working His remedy of restoration, bringing you the wonderful life He had intended by again bringing into harmony the spiritual and physical life. When things start to go well for you and your character begins to be transformed, you will see your life being renewed. This is His work.

Word Meanings: **Pneuma – Spirit:** the third person of the triune God, the Holy Spirit, coequal, coeternal with the Father and the Son
Kingdom: royal power, kingship, dominion, rule; not to be confused with an actual kingdom but rather the right or authority to rule over a kingdom; of the royal power of Jesus as the triumphant Messiah

LESSON 2:
WHY IS FAITH NECESSARY?

> - **Matthew 28:18-20:**
>
> [18] And Jesus came and said to them, "All authority in heaven and on earth has been given to me. + Go therefore and make disciples of all nations, baptizing them in[a] the name of the Father and of the Son and of the Holy Spirit,[20] teaching them to observe all that I have commanded you. And behold, I am with you always, to the end of the age."

_____
_____
_____
_____
_____

Word Meanings: **Authority:** Splendor, majesty, beauty, vigor, glory, in-charge, control, have jurisdiction, power to influence, cause to become: great; much; many; enlarged, exceedingly abundant, power (physical and spiritual) of doing supernatural. Right to govern, rule, command—possessing authority, mighty work, strength, miracle, performing miracles, excellence
Power: authority
Given: to grant, give to one asking, let have, to supply, furnish necessary things to give over, deliver

Christ said all the authority has been given to Him; and that He will be giving that to us as we teach others to live it out as we are living it out. We've already learned that without faith it is impossible to please Him. So, as we make disciples, we will be teaching them the same thing—to walk by faith, by receiving and exercising the life of authority—hearing and believing what He speaks.

> - **John 10:10:**
>
> [10] The thief comes only to steal and kill and destroy. I came that they may have life and have it abundantly.

LESSON 2:
WHY IS FAITH NECESSARY?

_____
_____
_____
_____
_____
_____

This life is one of exceeding abundance. It is restoration to the exceptional life that God gave Adam and Eve originally; a continual life of living by faith!

Word Meanings: **Have:** own, possess, hold firmly
Life: full, genuine, real, active, vigorous, fullness of life of God
Abundant: exceedingly, supremely, extraordinary, more remarkable, more excellent

> - **Isaiahh 61:1-4:**
>
> The Year of the Lord's Favor
> **61** The Spirit of the Lord God is upon me,
>   because the Lord has anointed me
> to bring good news to the poor;[a]
>   he has sent me to bind up the brokenhearted,
> to proclaim liberty to the captives,
>   and the opening of the prison to those who are bound;[b]
> ² to proclaim the year of the Lord's favor,
>   and the day of vengeance of our God;
>   to comfort all who mourn;
> ³ to grant to those who mourn in Zion—
>   to give them a beautiful headdress instead of ashes,
> the oil of gladness instead of mourning,
>   the garment of praise instead of a faint spirit;
> that they may be called oaks of righteousness,
>   the planting of the Lord, that he may be glorified.[c]
> ⁴ They shall build up the ancient ruins;
>   they shall raise up the former devastations;
> they shall repair the ruined cities,
>   the devastations of many generations.

LESSON 2:
WHY IS FAITH NECESSARY?

_____
_____
_____
_____
_____

No matter what has happened to us or what situation or difficulty we are in currently, or even what kind of adversity or pressure in which we find ourselves, the good news is that God can help us now. God can restore things now. God can provide His promised super-abundant life and bring resolution to the things we are facing now! Nothing is too difficult for Him, and our life is not relegated to His second, third or hundredth best. He can make all things work together for good, for His very best now, not later, or as many of us think, after this lifetime.

He speaks specifically to the conditions that tend to characterize our lives from things we have experienced or are experiencing now—for these He brings the good news of the super-abundant life that He promises. His promises are very specific. He assures us that He will deal with the issues of life that are resultant of the world of entropy and the work of the enemy. The super-abundant life is not a life of helping us manage these issues better or experiencing victory only once in a while, but then adding failure other times. He is instead offering true transformation: healing, liberty, beauty, joy, praise, true rebuilding—everything that characterizes the entirety of life. It will take time, but we will be transformed and will live the super-abundant life that He has come to give us. This is His promise to us. Our role is to learn how to abide in the Vine and receive His fruit, more fruit, much fruit. What a privilege!

Word Meanings:

Heal: bind up, repair
Liberty: free-flowing freedom
Open: release, give freedom
Comfort: bring compassion, console, hope
Beauty: ornaments, value
Joy: gladness, mirth (party)
Praise: thanksgiving, song in heart
Build: construct, rebuild, re-establish to original
Repair: make like new again

Since His Kingdom is spiritual and invisible, it requires faith to believe that the spiritual is superior to the physical and can work hand in hand with the physical in our lives. Read through these verses and again write down what we studied before regarding faith and what it is based upon.

LESSON 2:
WHY IS FAITH NECESSARY?

> - **Hebrews 11:1-3:**
>
> By Faith
> 11 Now faith is the assurance of things hoped for, the conviction of things not seen. 2 For by it the people of old received their commendation. 3 By faith we understand that the universe was created by the word of God, so that what is seen was not made out of things that are visible.

_____
_____
_____
_____
_____

To review, we saw the Scripture in verse three state that the world was created by what God spoke. So, the material and all of creation is subordinated or subject to the spiritual into the power of what God speaks. This means that your circumstances, since we operate in the natural, are subject to what God can fulfill through what He speaks. He can resolve, solve, or change anything supernaturally because the spiritual trumps the material. Thus, as we previously learned, He is the "I am" and nothing is too difficult for Him.

This means that God defines faith as the substance (something real) of things hoped for you (expected) and the evidence (certainty) of things not seen. As you ponder what is certain of things not seen (what will happen for sure that has not happened yet), we only have one answer—that which God speaks. God is trustworthy, and because what He speaks supersedes our circumstances, He defines faith as believing with certainty (absolutely no doubt) that what He has said will happen, though has not happened yet. The two elements of faith will thus be:

1. Do we have clarity about what He speaks?
2. Do we believe with certainty what He has spoken?

As we go through this course, we will continue to learn the depth and practical ways of learning these two elements.

LESSON 2:
WHY IS FAITH NECESSARY?

Word Meanings:

Faith: to be persuaded, to allow one's self to be persuaded; to be induced to believe: to have complete confidence in a thing

Substance: that which has foundation, is firm, that which has actual existence; a substance, real being—title deed, ownership

Hope: expectation of good, joy

Assurance/Conviction: a proof, that by which a thing is proved or tested, certainty; things: that which has been done, a deed, an accomplished fact; what is done or being accomplished

Not Seen: to perceive by the senses, to feel; to discover by use, to know by experience

Good Report: to be a witness, to bear witness, (i.e., to affirm that one has seen or heard or experienced something, or that he knows it because taught by the divine)

Framed: complete; to fit out, equip, put in order, arrange, adjust

Word of God: Rhema

Not Visible: to become evident, to be brought forth into the light, come to view

This glorifies God because He desires the invisible Kingdom to rule and bring about the Garden of Eden in our lives. Here, His kingdom is back in operation. Read through these verses and write down what is the essence of this Kingdom.

> - **John 11:40:**
>   40 Jesus said to her, "Did I not tell you that if you believed you would see the glory of God?"

_____
_____
_____
_____
_____

As we live in faith and experience the mighty power, the mighty work of God, we will see (bear witness to) the Glory of God. He will be demonstrating all that He wishes to do in, through, and around us, all as a result of our believing. He speaks what He will do—we hear, we receive, we then believe, and it happens. This is not about us, but about Him. He is glorified!

LESSON 2:
WHY IS FAITH NECESSARY?

Word Meanings: **Glory:** splendor, brightness, magnificence, excellence, preeminence, dignity, grace, majesty

We cannot please Him without this faith operating. Read through these verses and write out what they say about God's view of us operating without faith? Why is that important to us?

> - **Hebrews 10:38; Hebrews 11:6:**
>
>   ³⁸but my righteous one shall live by faith,
>   and if he shrinks back,
>   my soul has no pleasure in him."
>
>   ⁶ And without faith it is impossible to please him, for whoever would draw near to God must believe that he exists and that he rewards those who seek him.

_____
_____
_____
_____
_____

Remember, this is not as an arbitrary system, but because He wants us to experience this wonderful Kingdom life. It displeases Him that we miss out on this Kingdom because we have been walking by sight, figuring things out on our own, being limited to the physical, when there is a whole new kingdom life of the spiritual, one that can rule the physical.

Word Meanings: **Draw Back:** let down, lower, be timid, to withdraw
Not Pleased: not to be well pleased with, not take pleasure in, not to be favorably inclined toward one
Impossible: unable to be done, powerless, impotent

LESSON 2:
WHY IS FAITH NECESSARY?

Read through these verses and write down our purposes of living by faith in this fallen world. Why is this important to our life, and what does this mean about how we then are to live?

- **Ephesians 3:8-12:**
  [8] To me, though I am the very least of all the saints, this grace was given, to preach to the Gentiles the unsearchable riches of Christ, [9] and to bring to light for everyone what is the plan of the mystery hidden for ages in[a] God, who created all things, [10] so that through the church the manifold wisdom of God might now be made known to the rulers and authorities in the heavenly places. [11] This was according to the eternal purpose that he has realized in Christ Jesus our Lord, [12] in whom we have boldness and access with confidence through our faith in him.

_____
_____
_____
_____
_____

- **1 Samuel 2:35:**

  [35] And I will raise up for myself a faithful priest, who shall do according to what is in my heart and in my mind. And I will build him a sure house, and he shall go in and out before my anointed forever.

Word Meanings: **Heart:** mind, will, soul; mind: seat of emotions and passions

_____
_____
_____
_____
_____
_____

LESSON 2:
WHY IS FAITH NECESSARY?

This life of faith is for the true purpose of demonstrating that the material is again fully subject to the Spirit; bearing witness to principalities and powers that God's spiritual power is superior to the natural and are proven through us as we are both spiritual and physical. We are called as His priests who are to walk with Him by faith to know what is on His heart and mind, and then carry out His work by faith. In so doing, then He will be working through us performing His wonderful work in ways that only He can do; instead of us working on our own to do things naturally. By faith, we could have God's power supernaturally and would be given the gift of seeing what He can and will do.

Read through the following verses and write out the basis by which we have our relationship with God. Why is this important to us?

> - **1 John 1:5-8:**
>
>   Walking in the Light
>   ⁵ This is the message we have heard from him and proclaim to you, that God is light, and in him is no darkness at all. ⁶ If we say we have fellowship with him while we walk in darkness, we lie and do not practice the truth. ⁷ But if we walk in the light, as he is in the light, we have fellowship with one another, and the blood of Jesus his Son cleanses us from all sin. 8 If we say we have no sin, we deceive ourselves, and the truth is not in us.

_____
_____
_____
_____
_____

This makes us dependent and surrendered to Him. It requires us to walk in the Spirit and enjoy sweet fellowship with Him.

Word Meanings: **Fellowship:** association, community, communion, joint participation, intercourse, the share which one has in anything, participation, intimacy

LESSON 3:
WHY IS IT SO EASY TO LIVE WITHOUT FAITH, IN UNBELIEF?

Read through the following verses and write down the reasons we tend to operate by sight, in the natural and not live by faith? How do these affect us personally, and why are they so problematic?

Reasoning: Limited to the natural, intellect.

- **Mark 8:13-21:**

  [13] And he left them, got into the boat again, and went to the other side.

  The Leaven of the Pharisees and Herod
  [14] Now they had forgotten to bring bread, and they had only one loaf with them in the boat. [15] And he cautioned them, saying, "Watch out; beware of the leaven of the Pharisees and the leaven of Herod."[a] [16] And they began discussing with one another the fact that they had no bread. [17] And Jesus, aware of this, said to them, "Why are you discussing the fact that you have no bread? Do you not yet perceive or understand? Are your hearts hardened? [18] Having eyes do you not see, and having ears do you not hear? And do you not remember? [19] When I broke the five loaves for the five thousand, how many baskets full of broken pieces did you take up?" They said to him, "Twelve." [20] "And the seven for the four thousand, how many baskets full of broken pieces did you take up?" And they said to him, "Seven." [21] And he said to them, "Do you not yet understand?"

> "We go through a reasoning process that negates what God is promising and wind up wandering around outside of God's will, never experiencing the wonderful plan that He had in mind for us."

_____
_____
_____
_____
_____
_____

LESSON 3:
WHY IS IT SO EASY TO LIVE WITHOUT FAITH, IN UNBELIEF?

After the feeding of the four thousand, Jesus got in the boat with the disciples and made a statement: Beware of the Leaven of the Pharisees and of the Leaven of Herod. The disciples went to "reasoning" amongst themselves, actually thinking that Jesus was talking about the extra bread that they had forgotten to bring from the supernatural event they had just experienced. Jesus retorted that this was not about natural reasoning but about spiritual understanding; perceiving what He was speaking, which is the key to the beginning of processing faith. What is it that Christ is speaking? We are not to go to natural reasoning, thinking, and intellect, but rather spiritual discernment. The message Jesus wanted them to receive in this context was that they should be beware of the leaven (which needs only a little to grow, but then it permeates the whole; in this case our hearts and thinking) of the Pharisees (law, rules, and judgment) and of Herod (self-ambition and pleasure).

Word Meanings: **Reasoning:** to bring together different reasons, to reckon up the reasons, to reason, revolve in one's mind, deliberate

Not Perceive: not to think upon, heed, ponder, consider; not understand: not to set or join together in the mind

- **Numbers 14:1-4:**

  The People Rebel
  14 Then all the congregation raised a loud cry, and the people wept that night. ² And all the people of Israel grumbled against Moses and Aaron. The whole congregation said to them, "Would that we had died in the land of Egypt! Or would that we had died in this wilderness!³ Why is the Lord bringing us into this land, to fall by the sword? Our wives and our little ones will become a prey. Would it not be better for us to go back to Egypt?" ⁴ And they said to one another, "Let us choose a leader and go back to Egypt."

_____
_____
_____
_____
_____

LESSON 3:
WHY IS IT SO EASY TO LIVE WITHOUT FAITH, IN UNBELIEF?

After the Israelites crossed the Red Sea with Moses supernaturally, God spoke to them promising that He would give them the Promised Land—the land of Canaan—as their permanent home. It was a land of milk and honey with much bounty; and though occupied by a warrior nation, God would defeat them and then give them great peace and blessings. Twelve spies explored the Promised Land and returned with their report. Ten said that the enemy was too strong, had never been defeated, and it was not possible to succeed, regardless of what God had promised (even though they admitted to hearing God's promise). Joshua and Caleb, while agreeing with the assessment, had faith in God's words and urged the people to go forward in belief, expecting that God would do as He said (meaning He had given them a good report as seen in Hebrews 11:2). However, the report of the 10, called a bad report, prevailed, and the nation did not proceed because they refused to be persuaded that what God had to say was true (the very definition of unbelief). They grumbled and said four things that work against faith:

1. If only…we had made a different decision in the first place.

2. Why did we let God bring us to this point to actually cause us this trouble? (Here we see that they are now blaming God.) They reverse what they are to do and blame God for the trouble versus going forward with the promise that He had given them.

3. They reasoned they would be better off by coming up with their own plan.

4. They decided to act upon their own plan.

We go through a reasoning process that negates what God is promising and wind up wandering around outside of God's will, never experiencing the wonderful plan that He had in mind for us. Remember it is by His invitation, it is not automatic or by force.

Word Meanings:

Grumble: complain, murmur
If only!: thought of prior action being preferred, better course of action
Why: for what reason?, to what purpose?
Would It Not Be Better If: choice of alternative course of action being more successful
Good: pleasant, agreeable (to the senses); pleasant (to the higher nature), excellent, rich, valuable in estimation: glad, happy, prosperous
Let Us Appoint: give, bestow, grant, permit, ascribe, employ
Return: to turn back (from God), apostatize, to turn away

LESSON 3:
WHY IS IT SO EASY TO LIVE WITHOUT FAITH, IN UNBELIEF?

> - **Psalm 78:32-33:**
>
> ³² In spite of all this, they still sinned;
>   despite his wonders, they did not believe.
> ³³ So he made their days vanish like[a] a breath,[b]
>   and their years in terror.

_____
_____
_____
_____

Because we are unwilling to believe in His wondrous works, we are doomed to spend our days in futility—having no value and struggling to let Him show us the true meaning and importance of His plan. Instead, we experience feelings of worthlessness, all because we are unwilling to believe that He can show us wonder and amazing things for us personally.

Word Meanings: **Sinned:** to miss the mark; to induce to sin, cause to sin
Wondrous Works: to be marvelous, be wonderful, be surpassing, be extraordinary, separate by distinguishing action
Vanity: worthless, of no value
Trouble: calamity, dismay, ruin

We see in the following verses what happens when we focus on self, or desire for control, or choose rebellion, refusing to be persuaded that what God says is true:

> - **Deuteronomy 9:22-23:**
>
> ²² "At Taberah also, and at Massah and at Kibroth-hattaavah you provoked the Lord to wrath. ²³ And when the Lord sent you from Kadesh-barnea, saying, 'Go up and take possession of the land that I have given you,' then you rebelled against the commandment of the Lord your God and did not believe him or obey his voice."

_____
_____
_____
_____

LESSON 3:
WHY IS IT SO EASY TO LIVE WITHOUT FAITH, IN UNBELIEF?

Though instructed to go and possess the Promised Land, they rebelled and did not believe that they would be victorious, so did not obey; and thus, did not possess or enjoy the benefits of the possession of the Promised Land. Remember, unbelief is natural, but refusal to process this unbelief will have the dire consequence of us not receiving the faith needed to receive what God is promising.

Word Meanings:

Rebellious: to be contentious, be refractory, be disobedient toward, be rebellious against

Commandment: what God speaks to me

Hearkened: to hear with attention or interest, listen to; to understand, to consent, agree, yield to

---

- **Psalm 78:8-11:**

  [8] and that they should not be like their fathers,
      a stubborn and rebellious generation,
  a generation whose heart was not steadfast,
      whose spirit was not faithful to God.
  [9] The Ephraimites, armed with[a] the bow,
      turned back on the day of battle.
  [10] They did not keep God's covenant,
      but refused to walk according to his law.
  [11] They forgot his works
      and the wonders that he had shown them.

_____
_____
_____
_____
_____

This states that this generation did not seek God, were stubborn and rebellious, were not faithful, and though prepared for battle, turned back when things got tough. They did not pursue the Covenant (believe that they would be blessed to be a blessing) and refused to walk with God. Though God offered them the Covenant, because of fear and selfishness (and a desire to run their own lives), they chose to walk away from what God offered. As a result, they did not experience the Covenant blessings of God, which are received by faith.

LESSON 3:
WHY IS IT SO EASY TO LIVE WITHOUT FAITH, IN UNBELIEF?

Word Meanings: **Not Set Heart Aright:** not to be fixed, be securely determined, to be directed aright, be fixed aright, be steadfast (moral sense), to prepare, be ready, to be prepared, be arranged, be settled Steadfast: same word as believe

> - **Hebrews 3:15-19:**
>
> [15] As it is said,
> "Today, if you hear his voice,
> do not harden your hearts as in the rebellion."
> [16] For who were those who heard and yet rebelled? Was it not all those who left Egypt led by Moses? [17] And with whom was he provoked for forty years? Was it not with those who sinned, whose bodies fell in the wilderness? [18] And to whom did he swear that they would not enter his rest, but to those who were disobedient? [19] So we see that they were unable to enter because of unbelief.

_____
_____
_____
_____
_____

    As reviewed above in the Numbers passage, after the Israelites had crossed the Red Sea with Moses supernaturally, God spoke to them that He would give them the Promised Land—that He would defeat the enemy and provide to the nation a land of bounty and peace with great blessings. However, the people of the nation (about two million) rebelled, causing God to be angry with them for 40 years. They refused to proceed because they would not be persuaded that what God had to say was true (the very definition of unbelief)—so they could not enter the Promised Land. For 40 years they were never more than 11 miles from the Promised Land. They never again received another promise, and all died outside of God's will (except Joshua and Caleb, who believed). Remember that God's will is not guaranteed nor automatic, but instead is a life of walking by faith. We can live outside of God's will by refusing to be persuaded that what God says is true.

LESSON 3:
WHY IS IT SO EASY TO LIVE WITHOUT FAITH, IN UNBELIEF?

Word Meanings: **Sinned:** to err, be mistaken; to miss or wander from the path of uprightness and honor, to do or go wrong
Believed Not: refused to be persuaded that what God promised is true

- **Galatians: 5:19-21: Anger**

  [19] Now the works of the flesh are evident: sexual immorality, impurity, sensuality, [20] idolatry, sorcery, enmity, strife, jealousy, fits of anger, rivalries, dissensions, divisions, [21] envy,[a] drunkenness, orgies, and things like these. I warn you, as I warned you before, that those who do[b] such things will not inherit the kingdom of God.

_____
_____
_____
_____
_____

Some of the internal emotions that can keep us from walking in faith are anger, wrath, and bitterness. Though anger per se is not sin (and instead is a natural emotion), it can turn into sin if we do not resolve it quickly. When we allow this to happen, inevitably the anger captures our heart so that we are dominated by its effect. It is then that we no longer have the nature of Christ operating in us with freedom or the ability to hear and process faith. If we are captured by this, it will prevent us from living in faith.

Word Meanings: **Hatred:** enmity
Contention: strife, wrangling
Wrath: passion, angry, heat, anger forthwith boiling up and soon subsiding again, outbursts
Strife: a desire to put one's self forward, a partisan and fractious spirit

- **1 Samuel 17:10-11; 17:24-25: Fear:**

  [10] And the Philistine said, "I defy the ranks of Israel this day. Give me a man, that we may fight together." [11] When Saul and all Israel heard these words of the Philistine, they were dismayed and greatly afraid.

LESSON 3:
WHY IS IT SO EASY TO LIVE WITHOUT FAITH, IN UNBELIEF?

> ²⁴ All the men of Israel, when they saw the man, fled from him and were much afraid. ²⁵ And the men of Israel said, "Have you seen this man who has come up? Surely he has come up to defy Israel. And the king will enrich the man who kills him with great riches and will give him his daughter and make his father's house free in Israel."

_____
_____
_____
_____
_____

When Saul and his men were faced with the overwhelming prospect of being defeated by Goliath and the Philistines, their reaction was great fear and terror. The circumstances truly were overwhelming as the likely outcome in the natural was disaster. In these situations, fear (which is natural and okay) can prevent us from going to God to receive what He has to say to us (that we should have the faith to believe that God is with us) versus focusing on the potential awful outcome of living in great fear and terror.

Dismayed: to be shattered, be broken, be abolished, be afraid
Greatly Afraid: exceedingly terrified, in awe of wickedness and evil

- **Psalm 106:19-27: To actually despise the promises:**

    ¹⁹ They made a calf in Horeb
        and worshiped a metal image.
    ²⁰ They exchanged the glory of God[a]
        for the image of an ox that eats grass.
    ²¹ They forgot God, their Savior,
        who had done great things in Egypt,
    ²² wondrous works in the land of Ham,
        and awesome deeds by the Red Sea.
    ²³ Therefore he said he would destroy them—
        had not Moses, his chosen one,
    stood in the breach before him,

LESSON 3:
WHY IS IT SO EASY TO LIVE WITHOUT FAITH, IN UNBELIEF?

> to turn away his wrath from destroying them.
> ²⁴ Then they despised the pleasant land,
>   having no faith in his promise.
> ²⁵ They murmured in their tents,
>   and did not obey the voice of the Lord.
> ²⁶ Therefore he raised his hand and swore to them
>   that he would make them fall in the wilderness,
> ²⁷ and would make their offspring fall among the nations,
>   scattering them among the lands.

_____
_____
_____
_____
_____

After rebelling and refusing to be persuaded that what God had to say was true, the wanderers did not repent, but actually despised the promise. This is rather a funny thing. They blamed God for bringing them out of Egypt (which was where they experienced slavery and poverty) and chose not to follow Him and His will, and then wound up despising the very opportunity to live the grand life God had offered. So, in our refusal to learn to walk by faith, we can actually go deeper into the negative thinking of why bother, the promises are not real anyway. This can lead us to resent the possibilities of promises.

Word Meanings:

Forgot: ignore, wither, to cease to care
Despised: reject, disdain, abhor, refuse to pursue
Pleasant: precious, fantastic
Murmured: grumbled

- **John 5:37-40; 5:46-47: To not have His Word abiding in us:**

> ³⁷ And the Father who sent me has himself borne witness about me. His voice you have never heard, his form you have never seen, ³⁸ and you do not have his word abiding in you, for you do not believe the one whom he has sent. ³⁹ You

LESSON 3:
WHY IS IT SO EASY TO LIVE WITHOUT FAITH, IN UNBELIEF?

> search the Scriptures because you think that in them you have eternal life; and it is they that bear witness about me, [40] yet you refuse to come to me that you may have life.

_____
_____
_____
_____
_____

Jesus tells us that faith means that the Word abides in us as we abide in Him. If we are to live by faith, we first and foremost must be living a life of the Spirit, abiding in the relationship of the Vine, in Christ, and abiding in the Word as the Word is abiding in us. Without this, we will not be able to live by faith.

Word Meanings:

Word: Logos (not spending time in the Word)
Abiding: remaining, to continue to be present, to be held, kept, continually
What Moses Wrote: used of those things which stand written in the sacred books (of the Old Testament)
Graven Images: idols, things more important than God

- **Psalm 78:56-59: Idols:**

   [56] Yet they tested and rebelled against the Most High God
      and did not keep his testimonies,
   [57] but turned away and acted treacherously like their fathers;
      they twisted like a deceitful bow.
   [58] For they provoked him to anger with their high places;
      they moved him to jealousy with their idols.
   [59] When God heard, he was full of wrath,
      and he utterly rejected Israel.

As we see in these verses, one thing that gets in the way of us abiding is idols, those elements of life that become more important to us than walking with God. We put these ahead of wanting to know God, look to God, enjoy God, hear from God, trust God, etc. Idols will prevent us from going to faith and living out what He will be speaking to us.

LESSON 3:
WHY IS IT SO EASY TO LIVE WITHOUT FAITH, IN UNBELIEF?

Read the following verses in Psalms. We see here how we can get things backward. We want God to act, prior to us believing. This means we are testing Him to see if what He says is true.

- **Psalm 78:12-22; 78:40-42:**

12 In the sight of their fathers he performed wonders
   in the land of Egypt, in the fields of Zoan.
13 He divided the sea and let them pass through it,
   and made the waters stand like a heap.
14 In the daytime he led them with a cloud,
   and all the night with a fiery light.
15 He split rocks in the wilderness
   and gave them drink abundantly as from the deep.
16 He made streams come out of the rock
   and caused waters to flow down like rivers.
17 Yet they sinned still more against him,
   rebelling against the Most High in the desert.
18 They tested God in their heart
   by demanding the food they craved.
19 They spoke against God, saying,
   "Can God spread a table in the wilderness?
20 He struck the rock so that water gushed out
   and streams overflowed.
Can he also give bread
   or provide meat for his people?"
21 Therefore, when the Lord heard, he was full of wrath;
   a fire was kindled against Jacob;
   his anger rose against Israel,
22 because they did not believe in God
   and did not trust his saving power.

40 How often they rebelled against him in the wilderness
   and grieved him in the desert!
41 They tested God again and again
   and provoked the Holy One of Israel.
42 They did not remember his power[a]
   or the day when he redeemed them from the foe.

LESSON 3:
WHY IS IT SO EASY TO LIVE WITHOUT FAITH, IN UNBELIEF?

_____
_____
_____
_____
_____

This is one of the verses that many are confused about, and even backward. We tend to test God. We challenge God saying that if He really were a loving God, then He would do something important for me. This is often asked of God when people are having difficulty or trouble and are in need of a quick solution. Only then, will they believe/have faith in Him and what He is doing. He says He will wait longer than me, since He will not be tested, and we are getting it backward. Living by faith means that He speaks (His will), we receive, and then are to go to faith. (Do we believe what we hear?) Then when we believe, He will perform it. We cannot test Him. It actually limits His ability to work in our lives.

Word Meanings:

Provoked: to be contentious, be rebellious, be refractory, be disobedient toward, be rebellious against

Tempted: to test, try, prove, tempt, assay, put to the proof or test

Heart: inner man, mind, will, soul, understanding

Lust: seat of the appetites, seat of emotions and passions

Grieve: to hurt, pain, displease, vex, wrest

- **2 Chronicles 32:9-19: Work of Satan:**

Sennacherib Blasphemes
⁹ After this, Sennacherib king of Assyria, who was besieging Lachish with all his forces, sent his servants to Jerusalem to Hezekiah king of Judah and to all the people of Judah who were in Jerusalem, saying, ¹⁰ "Thus says Sennacherib king of Assyria, 'On what are you trusting, that you endure the siege in Jerusalem? ¹¹ Is not Hezekiah misleading you, that he may give you over to die by famine and by thirst, when he tells you, "The Lord our God will deliver us from the hand of the king of Assyria"? ¹² Has not this same Hezekiah taken away his high places and his altars and commanded Judah and Jerusalem, "Before one altar you shall worship, and on it you shall burn your sacrifices"? ¹³ Do you not know what I and my fathers have done to all the peoples of other lands? Were the gods of the nations of those lands at all able to deliver their lands

LESSON 3:
WHY IS IT SO EASY TO LIVE WITHOUT FAITH, IN UNBELIEF?

> out of my hand? ¹⁴ Who among all the gods of those nations that my fathers devoted to destruction was able to deliver his people from my hand, that your God should be able to deliver you from my hand? ¹⁵ Now, therefore, do not let Hezekiah deceive you or mislead you in this fashion, and do not believe him, for no god of any nation or kingdom has been able to deliver his people from my hand or from the hand of my fathers. How much less will your God deliver you out of my hand!'"
>
> ¹⁶ And his servants said still more against the Lord God and against his servant Hezekiah.¹⁷ And he wrote letters to cast contempt on the Lord, the God of Israel, and to speak against him, saying, "Like the gods of the nations of the lands who have not delivered their people from my hands, so the God of Hezekiah will not deliver his people from my hand." ¹⁸ And they shouted it with a loud voice in the language of Judah to the people of Jerusalem who were on the wall, to frighten and terrify them, in order that they might take the city. ¹⁹ And they spoke of the God of Jerusalem as they spoke of the gods of the peoples of the earth, which are the work of men's hands.

_____
_____
_____
_____
_____

Word Meanings:

Not Able to Deliver: not able to rescue, recover, to deliver (from enemies or troubles or death)
Make Afraid: to make exceedingly terrified, in awe of wickedness and evil

> - **2 Corinthians 4:3-4:**
>
> ³ And even if our gospel is veiled, it is veiled to those who are perishing. ⁴ In their case the god of this world has blinded the minds of the unbelievers, to keep them from seeing the light of the gospel of the glory of Christ, who is the image of God.

LESSON 3:
WHY IS IT SO EASY TO LIVE WITHOUT FAITH, IN UNBELIEF?

_____
_____
_____
_____
_____

The enemy wants to thwart God's will and is working to stop the process of us going to faith. When we recognize that the enemy is active in this process, we need to understand that by taking the authority given to us from God, we have a remedy to Satan's involvement. (We will review this further in a later chapter.)

Word Meanings: **Blinded:** to blunt the mental discernment, darken the mind
Minds: a mental perception, thought toward an evil purpose

LESSON 4:
WHAT ARE THE RESULTS OF UNBELIEF?

Unbelief is defined as the refusal to be persuaded that what God has to say is true. If we take this position and are not willing to process any further (either not willing to hear what He has to say in the first place, or keep processing until we get to faith), then the results will be dire.

Read through the following verses and write down the results of unbelief (the opposite of walking in faith) and how our lives will be affected by this unbelief.

> - **John 3:12: Not hear nor understand Heavenly things (the invisible powers of Heaven):**
>
> ¹² If I have told you earthly things and you do not believe, how can you believe if I tell you heavenly things?

Remember that without faith it is "impossible to please God."

_____
_____
_____
_____
_____
_____

Ignoring spiritual truths will shut off our hearing, deaden our spiritual discernment, and keep us from moving forward in receiving further promises from God. Remember that without faith it is "impossible to please God." This is not something arbitrary to prove God's authority over our lives, but instead something necessary for us to restore the spiritual and the physical to receive His grand, wonderful will for our lives, and for Him to demonstrate His great love for us.

LESSON 4:
WHAT ARE THE RESULTS OF UNBELIEF?

Word Meanings: **Earthly Things:** natural things that can be seen and observed
Heavenly Things: of heavenly origin or nature

- **Numbers 20:12: Not experience God's promises:**

    ¹² And the Lord said to Moses and Aaron, "Because you did not believe in me, to uphold me as holy in the eyes of the people of Israel, therefore you shall not bring this assembly into the land that I have given them."

_____
_____
_____
_____
_____

Word Meanings: **Not Enter:** not go in, come, go, come in

- **Isaiah 7:1-9:**

    Isaiah Sent to King Ahaz
    7 In the days of Ahaz the son of Jotham, son of Uzziah, king of Judah, Rezin the king of Syria and Pekah the son of Remaliah the king of Israel came up to Jerusalem to wage war against it, but could not yet mount an attack against it. ² When the house of David was told, "Syria is in league with[a] Ephraim," the heart of Ahaz[b] and the heart of his people shook as the trees of the forest shake before the wind.

    ³ And the Lord said to Isaiah, "Go out to meet Ahaz, you and Shear-jashub[c] your son, at the end of the conduit of the upper pool on the highway to the Washer's Field. ⁴ And say to him, 'Be careful, be quiet, do not fear, and do not let your heart be faint because of these two smoldering stumps of firebrands, at the fierce anger of Rezin and Syria and the son of Remaliah. ⁵ Because Syria, with

LESSON 4:
WHAT ARE THE RESULTS OF UNBELIEF?

> Ephraim and the son of Remaliah, has devised evil against you, saying, [6] "Let us go up against Judah and terrify it, and let us conquer it[d] for ourselves, and set up the son of Tabeel as king in the midst of it," [7] thus says the Lord God:
>
> "'It shall not stand,
>   and it shall not come to pass.
> [8] For the head of Syria is Damascus,
>   and the head of Damascus is Rezin.
> And within sixty-five years
>   Ephraim will be shattered from being a people.
> [9] And the head of Ephraim is Samaria,
>   and the head of Samaria is the son of Remaliah.
> If you[e] are not firm in faith,
>   you will not be firm at all.'"

_____
_____
_____
_____
_____

Word Meanings: **Not Be Established:** same word as not believe; so, if you do not believe, you will not be able to believe

- **Hebrews 3:19:**

  [19] So we see that they were unable to enter because of unbelief.

_____
_____
_____
_____
_____

LESSON 4:
WHAT ARE THE RESULTS OF UNBELIEF?

These verses say that we are actually prevented from experiencing and receiving God's promises, as these gifts are given through the believer's faith. If we refuse to enter a process of receiving faith by allowing Him to give us faith, we are then preventing God from delivering His promises to us. "They were not able to enter into the promised land because of their unbelief." It was not possible because they refused to be persuaded that what God had to say is true. They just stopped and said we are going no farther; they were unwilling for God to help them believe. So then, at that point of "stubbornness," God cannot deliver the promise anyway. It is offered by invitation not by force or automatically. And all we have to do is be willing to be persuaded—as He will do the work of giving us faith. His truth stands; and He is not arbitrary. He states that the life of faith is essential to receiving His promises. Since He will reward us with faith, we are actually refusing the reward, and rebelling against life with Him. Thus, the only way we prevent the wonderful life of promises and God's beautiful will is to be stubborn and unwilling to go further in the process of receiving faith.

- **Mark 16:14: Rebuked by God:**

  The Great Commission

  [14] Afterward he appeared to the eleven themselves as they were reclining at table, and he rebuked them for their unbelief and hardness of heart, because they had not believed those who saw him after he had risen.

_____
_____
_____
_____
_____

Word Meanings: **Rebuke:** to reproach, upbraid, revile

- **1 John 5:10-12:**

  [10] Whoever believes in the Son of God has the testimony in himself. Whoever does not believe God has made him a liar, because he has not believed in the

LESSON 4:
WHAT ARE THE RESULTS OF UNBELIEF?

> testimony that God has borne concerning his Son. ¹¹ And this is the testimony, that God gave us eternal life, and this life is in his Son. ¹² Whoever has the Son has life; whoever does not have the Son of God does not have life.

_____
_____
_____
_____
_____

Word Meanings: **Liar:** one who breaks faith, a false and faithless God

    By not walking by faith, He rebukes us as it makes Him out to be a liar, which He is not. We are presenting ourselves as children, as followers of Christ, but by refusing to walk by faith, He has no ability to deliver His life, His promises to us; and thus, we look just like the world—like a practical atheist—as though we are not believers. Our life is not representing God, which is why He rebukes us and says we are showing our life in Christ to be a lie.

> - **John 12:44-50: We will be judged by His words to us:**
>
> Jesus Came to Save the World
> ⁴⁴ And Jesus cried out and said, "Whoever believes in me, believes not in me but in him who sent me. ⁴⁵ And whoever sees me sees him who sent me. ⁴⁶ I have come into the world as light, so that whoever believes in me may not remain in darkness. ⁴⁷ If anyone hears my words and does not keep them, I do not judge him; for I did not come to judge the world but to save the world. ⁴⁸ The one who rejects me and does not receive my words has a judge; the word that I have spoken will judge him on the last day. ⁴⁹ For I have not spoken on my own authority, but the Father who sent me has himself given me a commandment—what to say and what to speak. ⁵⁰ And I know that his commandment is eternal life. What I say, therefore, I say as the Father has told me."

LESSON 4:
WHAT ARE THE RESULTS OF UNBELIEF?

_____
_____
_____
_____
_____

Christ says He has not come to judge, but rather His words, His truth will judge us. His words stand on their own and are a double-edged sword: If believing and following His word creates and delivers the promises, but we refuse to believe and follow, He and His words cannot deliver the promise—and we suffer the consequences. The Word is not partial or arbitrary, but wholly true. This is why that which He speaks to us as His word is to be received and then taken to faith; and not rejected by refusing to believe them as being true.

Word Meanings:

Words: Rhema
Rejected: to do away with, to set aside, disregard, to thwart the efficacy of anything, nullify, make void, frustrate
Not Receive: not to take up a thing to be carried, not to take upon one's self
Judge: to pronounce an opinion, a ruling concerning right and wrong

> - **Psalm 78:41: Limit His power, restrict the miraculous:**
>
>   ⁴¹ They tested God again and again
>   and provoked the Holy One of Israel.

_____
_____
_____
_____
_____

Word Meanings: **Limited:** restricted

51

LESSON 4:
WHAT ARE THE RESULTS OF UNBELIEF?

> - **Matthew 13:58:**
>
> ⁵⁸ And he did not do many mighty works there, because of their unbelief.

_____
_____
_____
_____
_____

Word Meanings: **Mighty Works:** power for performing miracles

> - **Mark 6:5-6:**
>
> ⁵ And he could do no mighty work there, except that he laid his hands on a few sick people and healed them. ⁶ And he marveled because of their unbelief. And he went about among the villages teaching.

_____
_____
_____
_____
_____

Word Meanings: **Marveled at:** to wonder, wonder at, could not fathom

Unbelief limits what God can do. Jesus could not (though He wanted to and obviously had the power to) accomplish any or many miracles where there was unbelief. The power of faith unleashes His power and fulfillment of His will. Unbelief limits and diminishes this power and fulfillment. Remember that God's definition of unbelief is "refusal to be persuaded that what He says He will do is true; or even experience that what He does is true." This is what limits and diminishes His power to act and fulfill what He has planned in our life. By definition, all of us begin our journey in learning how to walk in faith as "neophytes" with little understanding or experience. We all need persuading and

LESSON 4:
WHAT ARE THE RESULTS OF UNBELIEF?

to be shown His power. Think of the disciples. They all were challenged with: "Come and follow Me" and knew nothing of faith. Jesus continued to perform amazing miracles such as the feeding of the 5,000, turning water into wine, etc. It took three years for these men to receive what it meant to walk in faith. Though they did not "believe" and in fact many times, Jesus challenged them with: "O ye of little faith," they did not limit or diminish His power. So, what is the difference? They never refused to be persuaded that what He was doing or what He said was true. They struggled with understanding it, and did not immediately have the confidence of faith to believe it, but they never refused to be persuaded by walking away from it. This is the very definition of unbelief; and why it will prevent us from going any further in our journey of faith.

LESSON 5:
HOW DO WE OPERATE IN FAITH?

So, how do we operate by walking in faith? Read through the following verses and write down the keys to operating in faith. What are the truths to how we receive faith and how we live by faith? How would we then live this faith in our daily lives?

> - **Hebrews 12:1-2: Understand Christ is the author and finisher of faith:**
>
> Jesus, Founder and Perfecter of Our Faith
> **12** Therefore, since we are surrounded by so great a cloud of witnesses, let us also lay aside every weight, and sin which clings so closely, and let us run with endurance the race that is set before us, ² looking to Jesus, the founder and perfecter of our faith, who for the joy that was set before him endured the cross, despising the shame, and is seated at the right hand of the throne of God.

> "Christ is the author and finisher of faith; He authors faith by starting it. He starts it by speaking a Word, a promise to us."

_____
_____
_____
_____
_____

Christ is the author and finisher of faith; He authors faith by starting it. He starts it by speaking a Word, a promise to us. We ask Him: What do you have to say to us? He speaks it through a verse(s) and through application of personal statements to us that reveal His secrets to us. Then He is the finisher, which means that after He starts it with His Word to us, He has to take it to certainty. (We are certain it will happen as He spoke it, regardless of any circumstances to the contrary.) It is His work from beginning to end. It is not our own hard work, but a process that He offers to us.

LESSON 5:
HOW DO WE OPERATE IN FAITH?

Word Meanings: **Author:** one who takes the lead in anything and thus affords an example, a predecessor in a matter, pioneer

Finisher: a perfecter, one who has in his own person raised faith to its perfection and so set before us the highest example of faith

> - **Hebrews 11:6: Know that He is "I Am" and diligently seek Him:**
>
> ⁶ And without faith it is impossible to please him, for whoever would draw near to God must believe that he exists and that he rewards those who seek him.

_____
_____
_____
_____
_____

Our basic role in faith is meeting two conditions:

1. Believe that He is the "I Am" (not that He is, as in the English translation, which we all do, no problem). Believing He is the "I Am" means that we have settled that He is the Almighty God who is able to handle anything in our lives—any situation, any circumstance, any trouble, any difficulty, and any challenge. So, when He speaks His promise to me, I will receive it because I have settled that nothing is too difficult for Him. I am to receive it willingly and then process it through to certainty. He is authoring this to me, so I am not going to reject this Word.

2. Diligently seek Him (stay with Him through the entire process) with a heart of joy and persistence, and do not give up or get lazy. Remember and know that He will reward me with what I need—faith.

Word Meanings: **Rewarder:** one who pays wages

Diligently Seek: search for carefully

LESSON 5:
HOW DO WE OPERATE IN FAITH?

> - **Galatians 3:13-18: Must remain in Christ, through whom promises become realized:**
>
> [13] Christ redeemed us from the curse of the law by becoming a curse for us—for it is written, "Cursed is everyone who is hanged on a tree"— [14] so that in Christ Jesus the blessing of Abraham might come to the Gentiles, so that we might receive the promised Spirit[a] through faith.
>
> The Law and the Promise
> [15] To give a human example, brothers:[b] even with a man-made covenant, no one annuls it or adds to it once it has been ratified. [16] Now the promises were made to Abraham and to his offspring. It does not say, "And to offsprings," referring to many, but referring to one, "And to your offspring," who is Christ. [17] This is what I mean: the law, which came 430 years afterward, does not annul a covenant previously ratified by God, so as to make the promise void. [18] For if the inheritance comes by the law, it no longer comes by promise; but God gave it to Abraham by a promise.

_____
_____
_____
_____
_____

    This is an interesting truth: The promises are not actually available to those of us who are seeds of Abraham. Instead, they are available only to Christ: the SEED of Abraham. He is the only recipient. As the recipient, He then gives those promises to us, as we live in, remain in, and stay in Him. As we do, we realize those promises. Why? He is the author and finisher of faith, so it is imperative that we stay in process with Him from beginning to end. We should enjoy His work as the author and finisher, the one who both gives us faith, and then fulfills His promises to us.

Word Meanings:

Blessing of Abraham: a (concrete) blessing, benefit
Receive: to take up a thing to be carried, to take upon one's self
Promise: a promised good or blessing (Covenant)
Seed: the grain or kernel which contains within itself the germ of the future plants

LESSON 5:
HOW DO WE OPERATE IN FAITH?

> - **2 Corinthians 1:18-24: Understand that all the promises of God are YES:**
>
> [18] As surely as God is faithful, our word to you has not been Yes and No. [19] For the Son of God, Jesus Christ, whom we proclaimed among you, Silvanus and Timothy and I, was not Yes and No, but in him it is always Yes. [20] For all the promises of God find their Yes in him. That is why it is through him that we utter our Amen to God for his glory. [21] And it is God who establishes us with you in Christ, and has anointed us, [22] and who has also put his seal on us and given us his Spirit in our hearts as a guarantee.[a]
>
> [23] But I call God to witness against me—it was to spare you that I refrained from coming again to Corinth. 24 Not that we lord it over your faith, but we work with you for your joy, for you stand firm in your faith.

_____
_____
_____
_____
_____

    Paul states that ALL the promises of God (over 7,000 in Scriptures) are not yes and no—meaning perhaps, maybe, subject to the whim of God, the luck of the draw, etc.—but are YES in Christ Jesus. When He speaks these to us (remember, all promises from Him must be spoken to us by Him; we cannot take them as we wish, which, by definition, means we would then be operating in the self), we can count on them being absolutely true and always answered with YES. When these are spoken to us, and since they are ALL yes, our response should always be AMEN, which in the Hebrew means: "I have heard this personal promise to me, I receive this as being true for me, and now, yes, amen, so be it. May you perform it as you have promised."

Word Meanings:

Yes: verily, truly, assuredly, even so
Promise: a promised good or blessing (Covenant)
Amen: at the end, so it is, so be it, may it be fulfilled. It was a custom, which passed over from the synagogues to the Christian assemblies, that when he who had read or discoursed had offered up solemn prayer to God, the others responded amen, and thus made the substance of what was uttered their own.

LESSON 5:
HOW DO WE OPERATE IN FAITH?

> - **Romans 4:17-21: Be in His presence and be willing to be persuaded. Fight against losing hope in impossible circumstances:**
>
> [17] as it is written, "I have made you the father of many nations"—in the presence of the God in whom he believed, who gives life to the dead and calls into existence the things that do not exist. [18] In hope he believed against hope, that he should become the father of many nations, as he had been told, "So shall your offspring be." [19] He did not weaken in faith when he considered his own body, which was as good as dead (since he was about a hundred years old), or when he considered the barrenness[a] of Sarah's womb. [20] No unbelief made him waver concerning the promise of God, but he grew strong in his faith as he gave glory to God, [21] fully convinced that God was able to do what he had promised.

_____
_____
_____
_____

Abraham was identified by Paul as a great man of faith. As we know, for much of his life, though, Abraham had trouble (indeed, failed!) believing. We know that he tried to sell his wife twice when he was afraid for his life, and we also know that he and Sarah took things into their own hands (Hagar/Ismael) when it looked like they would not be successful in having a child (even though it had been promised by God). Eventually, though, Abraham allowed himself to believe. He wound up being a great man of faith and proved this when God asked him to sacrifice his son, Isaac, the son of promise. (Abraham stated that he and the boy would return down the mountain, as he believed that God would bring him back from the dead, he was so sure of the promise given: Hebrews 11:19).

We know that God provided a substitute sacrifice to Abraham, which was a foreshadow of Christ substitutionary atonement. Verse 21 says that Abraham was persuaded that God would perform what He said. The key word here is persuaded. As we discussed above, the disciples (as they were first called) needed to be persuaded that what Jesus spoke would happen; and even into the second and third year of Christ's ministry, they still struggled with faith. It wasn't until after Pentecost they were fully persuaded that what God spoke through the Holy Spirit would be performed (they then lived by faith and saw great and mighty things done in and through their lives). Like Abraham, then, we need to stay with God

LESSON 5:
HOW DO WE OPERATE IN FAITH?

through the process and be willing to see whatever it is He is revealing to us. For this, we must be willing to live in faith.

Word Meanings:
Weak: feeble, to be without strength, powerless
Not Consider: not consider attentively or fix one's eyes or mind upon
Wavered Not: not to be at variance with one's self, hesitate, doubt
Strengthened: to receive strength, be strengthened, increase in strength
Persuaded: fully convinced or assured
Perform: to a promise

- **John 14:10-11: Be watching for and receive His supernatural works in your life that are meant to build confidence (do not require faith):**

  [10] Do you not believe that I am in the Father and the Father is in me? The words that I say to you I do not speak on my own authority, but the Father who dwells in me does his works. [11] Believe me that I am in the Father and the Father is in me, or else believe on account of the works themselves.

_____
_____
_____
_____
_____

Word Meanings:
Word: Rhema
Works: that which one undertakes to do, enterprise, undertaking
Sake: in agreement

- **John 10:25; 10:37-38:**
  [25] Jesus answered them, "I told you, and you do not believe. The works that I do in my Father's name bear witness about me…

  [37] If I am not doing the works of my Father, then do not believe me; [38] but if I do them, even though you do not believe me, believe the works, that you may know and understand that the Father is in me and I am in the Father."

LESSON 5:
HOW DO WE OPERATE IN FAITH?

Word Meanings:

Bear Witness: to affirm that one has seen or heard or experienced something, or that he knows it because taught by divine revelation or inspiration

Know: understand, perceive, have knowledge of, to understand, intimate experience with

Believe: to think to be true, to be persuaded of, to credit, place confidence in

> - **John 14:29:**
>
>   [29] And now I have told you before it takes place, so that when it does take place you may believe.

Word Meanings:

Come to Pass: to become, happen

Believe: to think to be true, to be persuaded of, to credit, place confidence in

    As we are being persuaded, He asks us to believe in the works themselves that He will be doing to demonstrate His power and might. We should be observing what He is doing and be open to the mighty and wonderful things He demonstrates to us as these show us the reality and thus the continued possibilities of the supernatural that He wants us to believe more and more. Even when it is a struggle to believe, be watching for and observing the amazing things that He will do to persuade and bear witness to His power and wonder for us.

LESSON 5:
HOW DO WE OPERATE IN FAITH?

- **James 1:5-8: Ask for help:**

    5 If any of you lacks wisdom, let him ask God, who gives generously to all without reproach, and it will be given him. 6 But let him ask in faith, with no doubting, for the one who doubts is like a wave of the sea that is driven and tossed by the wind. For that person must not suppose that he will receive anything from the Lord; 8 he is a double-minded man, unstable in all his ways.

_____
_____
_____
_____
_____

Word Meanings: **Ask:** beg, call for, crave, desire, require
Liberally: simply, openly, frankly, sincerely
Faith: conviction of the truth of anything, belief
Doubting: to oppose, strive with dispute, contend

- **1 Corinthians 2:2-5:**

    2 For I decided to know nothing among you except Jesus Christ and him crucified. 3 And I was with you in weakness and in fear and much trembling, 4 and my speech and my message were not in plausible words of wisdom, but in demonstration of the Spirit and of power, 5 so that your faith might not rest in the wisdom of men[a] but in the power of God.

_____
_____
_____
_____
_____

LESSON 5:
HOW DO WE OPERATE IN FAITH?

Word Meanings: **Manifest:** showing forth, a demonstration, proof
Power: power for performing miracles
Wisdom of Men: specifically the varied knowledge of things human and divine, acquired by acuteness and experience

- **Mark 9:14-24:**

  Jesus Heals a Boy with an Unclean Spirit
  14 And when they came to the disciples, they saw a great crowd around them, and scribes arguing with them. 15 And immediately all the crowd, when they saw him, were greatly amazed and ran up to him and greeted him. 16 And he asked them, "What are you arguing about with them?" 17 And someone from the crowd answered him, "Teacher, I brought my son to you, for he has a spirit that makes him mute. 18 And whenever it seizes him, it throws him down, and he foams and grinds his teeth and becomes rigid. So I asked your disciples to cast it out, and they were not able." 19 And he answered them, "O faithless generation, how long am I to be with you? How long am I to bear with you? Bring him to me." 20 And they brought the boy to him. And when the spirit saw him, immediately it convulsed the boy, and he fell on the ground and rolled about, foaming at the mouth. 21 And Jesus asked his father, "How long has this been happening to him?" And he said, "From childhood. 22 And it has often cast him into fire and into water, to destroy him. But if you can do anything, have compassion on us and help us." 23 And Jesus said to him, "'If you can'! All things are possible for one who believes." 24 Immediately the father of the child cried out[a] and said, "I believe; help my unbelief!"

_____
_____
_____
_____
_____

Word Meanings: **Help:** bring aid

LESSON 5:
HOW DO WE OPERATE IN FAITH?

> - **Luke 17:5-6: Just need a little (mustard seed) to begin:**
>
> Increase Our Faith
> ⁵ The apostles said to the Lord, "Increase our faith!" ⁶ And the Lord said, "If you had faith like a grain of mustard seed, you could say to this mulberry tree, 'Be uprooted and planted in the sea,' and it would obey you.

_____
_____
_____
_____
_____

Word Meanings:

Increase: to add
Mustard: the name of a plant, which in Asian countries grows from a very small seed and attains to the height of a tree, 10 feet (three meters) and more; hence a very small quantity of a thing is likened to a mustard seed, and also a thing that grows to a remarkable size

God understands that we need help to have faith. We need wisdom, insight, assistance with doubt, and the power to believe (especially that portion of your unbelief that is transformed to faith). Instead of refusing to go further, or trying to figure this all out on our own, or struggling to work at having more faith, we are instead to go to Him and ask Him to help our unbelief; to give us the spiritual understanding regarding blockages, heart issues, past experiences, etc. and the life of the Word to overcome and bring us to certainty. Stay with it, stay with it, stay with it. When you ask Him to help you with your unbelief, He will.

LESSON 6:
HOW DO WE OPERATE IN FAITH? (CONTINUED)

As you did in Session 5, continue to read through the following verses and write down the keys to operating in faith? What are the truths to how we receive faith and live by faith? How would we then live this out?

> - **1 Thessalonians 2:13: Abide in the Word, hear and receive His Word:**
>
> 13 And we also thank God constantly[a] for this, that when you received the word of God, which you heard from us, you accepted it not as the word of men[b] but as what it really is, the word of God, which is at work in you believers.

_____
_____
_____
_____
_____

Word Meanings:

Received: to take to, to take with one's self, to join to one's self
Word: Logos
Truth: truly, of a truth, in reality, most certainly
Effectively Works: to be operative, be at work, put forth power

> - **Romans 10:8, 10:17:**
> 8 But what does it say? "The word is near you, in your mouth and in your heart" (that is, the word of faith that we proclaim);
>
> 17 So faith comes from hearing, and hearing through the word of Christ.

LESSON 6:
HOW DO WE OPERATE IN FAITH? (CONTINUED)

Word Meanings: **Word:** Rhema
Heart: the center and seat of spiritual life, the soul or mind, as it is the fountain and seat of the thoughts, passions, desires, appetites, affections, purposes, endeavors, of the understanding, the faculty and seat of the intelligence, of the will and character, of the soul so far as it is affected and stirred in a bad way or good, or of the soul as the seat of the sensibilities, affections, emotions, desires, appetites, passions

Faith comes from hearing the Word. When we diligently seek Him, we are to abide, abide, abide in the Word – stay focused on the Word that He has spoken to us, always remembering what has been promised. Do we believe it? Why or why not? Dialogue with God about seeking strength to believe it; receiving more insight, wisdom, truth about this Word that He has given us. We are to stay with this until we are certain that what He has spoken is now settled in our heart. We are not to focus on the circumstances, the problems, the issues of what is causing us to doubt (it is okay to dialogue with God about them, but not to focus or spend all of our time thinking about those or coming up with our own plans). Recall those things that prevent faith and keep receiving what He has spoken in the Word. This is the nature of true abiding.

- **Jude 1:20: Pray in the Spirit:**

    [20] But you, beloved, building yourselves up in your most holy faith and praying in the Holy Spirit…

LESSON 6:
HOW DO WE OPERATE IN FAITH? (CONTINUED)

Word Meanings: **Build Up Faith:** increase, add to

> - **2 Thessalonians 1:11:**
>
>   [11] To this end we always pray for you, that our God may make you worthy of his calling and may fulfill every resolve for good and every work of faith by his power…

_____
_____
_____
_____
_____

Word Meanings: **Pleasure:** good will, kindly intent, benevolence

> - **Philippians 1:6:**
>
>   [6] And I am sure of this, that he who began a good work in you will bring it to completion at the day of Jesus Christ.

_____
_____
_____
_____
_____

Word Meanings: **Good:** pleasant, agreeable, joyful, happy, excellent, distinguished, upright, honorable
Work: that which one undertakes to do, enterprise, undertaking
Perform: to bring to an end, accomplish, perfect, execute, complete

LESSON 6:
HOW DO WE OPERATE IN FAITH? (CONTINUED)

As we are abiding in the Word, we further pray these promises given to us personally and pray in the Spirit that He would:

1. Build us up and give us the faith to believe these personal promises, which is the very reward He promises to us as we continue to stay in process with Him.

2. Work His power according to His good pleasure as we glorify the name of Christ in us through Him taking us to faith in the promises personally given to us. We should always be willing to be persuaded that what He says He will perform.

3. Complete the work that He has begun. There are two works that are ongoing:
    a. The work of faith that He authored (by speaking His Word to us) and will finish (taking faith to me, so that I fully believe it).
    b. Then, fulfill the promise of what He has spoken, which translates into changed circumstances as He does something amazing in my life, (i.e., His work).

We pray, pray, pray. Do this together with abiding and stay in process. This is a privilege of our relationship and is the way that He finishes faith in us.

- **2 Chronicles 20:1-21: Pray and fast; gather in unity; ask for help; hear; respond in obedience:**

    Jehoshaphat's Prayer
    20 After this the Moabites and Ammonites, and with them some of the Meunites,[a] came against Jehoshaphat for battle. ² Some men came and told Jehoshaphat, "A great multitude is coming against you from Edom,[b] from beyond the sea; and, behold, they are in Hazazon-tamar" (that is, Engedi). ³ Then Jehoshaphat was afraid and set his face to seek the Lord, and proclaimed a fast throughout all Judah. ⁴ And Judah assembled to seek help from the Lord; from all the cities of Judah they came to seek the Lord.

LESSON 6:
HOW DO WE OPERATE IN FAITH? (CONTINUED)

5 And Jehoshaphat stood in the assembly of Judah and Jerusalem, in the house of the Lord, before the new court, 6 and said, "O Lord, God of our fathers, are you not God in heaven? You rule over all the kingdoms of the nations. In your hand are power and might, so that none is able to withstand you. 7 Did you not, our God, drive out the inhabitants of this land before your people Israel, and give it forever to the descendants of Abraham your friend? 8 And they have lived in it and have built for you in it a sanctuary for your name, saying, 9 'If disaster comes upon us, the sword, judgment,[c] or pestilence, or famine, we will stand before this house and before you—for your name is in this house—and cry out to you in our affliction, and you will hear and save.' 10 And now behold, the men of Ammon and Moab and Mount Seir, whom you would not let Israel invade when they came from the land of Egypt, and whom they avoided and did not destroy— 11 behold, they reward us by coming to drive us out of your possession, which you have given us to inherit. 12 O our God, will you not execute judgment on them? For we are powerless against this great horde that is coming against us. We do not know what to do, but our eyes are on you."

13 Meanwhile all Judah stood before the Lord, with their little ones, their wives, and their children. 14 And the Spirit of the Lord came[d] upon Jahaziel the son of Zechariah, son of Benaiah, son of Jeiel, son of Mattaniah, a Levite of the sons of Asaph, in the midst of the assembly. 15 And he said, "Listen, all Judah and inhabitants of Jerusalem and King Jehoshaphat: Thus says the Lord to you, 'Do not be afraid and do not be dismayed at this great horde, for the battle is not yours but God's. 16 Tomorrow go down against them. Behold, they will come up by the ascent of Ziz. You will find them at the end of the valley, east of the wilderness of Jeruel. 17 You will not need to fight in this battle. Stand firm, hold your position, and see the salvation of the Lord on your behalf, O Judah and Jerusalem.' Do not be afraid and do not be dismayed. Tomorrow go out against them, and the Lord will be with you."

18 Then Jehoshaphat bowed his head with his face to the ground, and all Judah and the inhabitants of Jerusalem fell down before the Lord, worshiping the Lord. 19 And the Levites, of the Kohathites and the Korahites, stood up to praise the Lord, the God of Israel, with a very loud voice.

20 And they rose early in the morning and went out into the wilderness of Tekoa. And when they went out, Jehoshaphat stood and said, "Hear me, Judah and inhabitants of Jerusalem! Believe in the Lord your God, and you will be

LESSON 6:
HOW DO WE OPERATE IN FAITH? (CONTINUED)

> established; believe his prophets, and you will succeed." 21 And when he had taken counsel with the people, he appointed those who were to sing to the Lord and praise him in holy attire, as they went before the army, and say,
>
> "Give thanks to the Lord,
>   for his steadfast love endures forever."

_____
_____
_____
_____
_____

Jehoshaphat had the armies of Moab, Ammon, and "others"—great multitudes coming against them. The armies were on their way and irreversible. In those days, battles were primarily won by pure numbers; the armies with the largest number of men won the battle and defeated the nation with the fewer number of men in battle. In this case, because of the overwhelming alliance of these three-plus armies coming together, Israel and Jehoshaphat, based upon the "natural cause and effect of the circumstances," had no chance. They were going to be defeated and, in fact, wiped out.

What did Jehoshaphat do? He did fear as he could not ignore the reality of what was happening. But importantly, he did not allow himself to go to either end of the believer's spectrum: on one side giving up and on the other side trusting God and seeing what might happen (today called Christian fatalism). Instead, and with the reality of fear (which is normal and okay), he purposely "set himself to seek the Lord," and gathered the nation (other believers who also were willing to seek God) with him. Here is how he sought the Lord:

1. He stood on the promises/truths he already knew based on the time he had spent "abiding in" what had been written in the Torah and was revealed by the prophets; he knew and understood those truths were truly from God. He had understood through the Covenant to Abraham and then reiterated to Moses and to David that God would protect Israel; that even in extreme difficulty God would save them. He stood on these promises as his starting point of seeking the Lord. He did not ask God, "Are you going to save us?" He already believed that what God had spoken was still true for him and his people as children of God.

LESSON 6:
HOW DO WE OPERATE IN FAITH? (CONTINUED)

2. Then, based upon these promises, he sought God in this circumstance, asking God's solution to his problem. He shared with God that he did not know what to do, so he inquired:

    a) What are you going to do?
    b) What do you want us to do?

3. As they stood on the promise and then sought personal wisdom, God answered: "The battle is not yours but mine. Go down tomorrow armed up for battle to a specific location and watch what I will do to deliver you." They received their personal wisdom to this particular crisis (Rhema).

4. Jehoshaphat did as God instructed and said to his people, "Believe the prophets (the promise that we stood on) and believe what God has said (our wisdom, our Rhema) and we will be both established and successful. All of this will happen just as God said. So, the promise was potential but not guaranteed—it took faith, and it took obedience.

5. And it all happened as God stated. The enemy was defeated and in fact, because the enemy was so sure they were going to win, they brought all their valuables with them; and thus, Jehoshaphat and his people took three days to carry it all back. What had started as a crisis turned into a great blessing.

What, then, do we do when we find ourselves in crisis, when our work and life are greatly affected? First, remember that it is acceptable and normal to be afraid. In life, things are happening and going to come against us. Remember the promises of God that are true for us and abide in what is true. In Psalm 91, we read God's question to us: "Do you believe in my promises?" Then at the end of the Psalm, He says: "Call to Me, and I will answer you." The truth of this promise reminds us never to give up or go to Christian fatalism. Instead, seek His personal wisdom, which will reveal both what He is going to do and what He wants you to do. You can be assured He will guide you and lead you onto the path He has planned out.

Word Meanings: **Seek:** to resort to, seek with care, enquire, require
Gathered Together: in unity
Ask: request help
Stand: take one's stand, be in a standing attitude, stand forth, take a stand, present oneself, attend upon, be or become servant of
Believe: be established (same Hebrew words), believe and will be able to believe
Prosper: advance, make progress, succeed, be profitable

LESSON 6:
HOW DO WE OPERATE IN FAITH? (CONTINUED)

- **Ephesians 4:1-16: Go to unity with others who are willing to believe:**

Unity in the Body of Christ

4 I therefore, a prisoner for the Lord, urge you to walk in a manner worthy of the calling to which you have been called, ² with all humility and gentleness, with patience, bearing with one another in love, ³ eager to maintain the unity of the Spirit in the bond of peace. ⁴ There is one body and one Spirit—just as you were called to the one hope that belongs to your call—⁵ one Lord, one faith, one baptism, ⁶ one God and Father of all, who is over all and through all and in all. ⁷ But grace was given to each one of us according to the measure of Christ's gift.⁸ Therefore it says,

"When he ascended on high he led a host of captives,
      and he gave gifts to men."[a]

⁹ (In saying, "He ascended," what does it mean but that he had also descended into the lower regions, the earth?[b] ¹⁰ He who descended is the one who also ascended far above all the heavens, that he might fill all things.) ¹¹ And he gave the apostles, the prophets, the evangelists, the shepherds[c] and teachers,[d] ¹² to equip the saints for the work of ministry, for building up the body of Christ, ¹³ until we all attain to the unity of the faith and of the knowledge of the Son of God, to mature manhood,[e] to the measure of the stature of the fullness of Christ, ¹⁴ so that we may no longer be children, tossed to and fro by the waves and carried about by every wind of doctrine, by human cunning, by craftiness in deceitful schemes. ¹⁵ Rather, speaking the truth in love, we are to grow up in every way into him who is the head, into Christ, ¹⁶ from whom the whole body, joined and held together by every joint with which it is equipped, when each part is working properly, makes the body grow so that it builds itself up in love.

_____
_____
_____
_____

LESSON 6:
HOW DO WE OPERATE IN FAITH? (CONTINUED)

When we reach unity, we must remember there are three parties involved: you, your spouse (or believing friend), and the Holy Spirit. We are not to negotiate settlements and reach agreement in the flesh but rather to discover God's will together, and then come to unity with God through the Holy Spirit. The wonderful thing about this process is that we can reach unity 100 percent, all the time, because of the promise given to us by God. He will always reveal His will to us. The same Spirit is within me and my spouse or another believing friend. If we have a willingness to work through the process, He will reveal to both of us His will. That is why He asked us to make every effort (work hard at this) to get to unity with and through the Spirit. Another beautiful thing about this process is that this agreement is normal and expected.

We are to embrace and honor disagreement, to understand that neither of us knows God's will and that together, through the disagreement, we are now to pursue and work hard to receive God's will. Three possibilities for Him to bring resolution will be:

1. for Him to change my heart and see that what my spouse or friend is seeing is in line with God's will

2. for Him to change my spouse's or my friend's heart to see that what I am seeing is in line with God's will

3. that neither one of us is seeing what is in line with God's will and more is to be discovered before we know God's will. We need to keep asking, seeking, and knocking. Instead of arguing and manipulating disagreements, our heart is to work toward unity as we seek God's will together. Remember that God commands blessing. Why would we not work toward that blessing?

As we saw above in the example of Jehoshaphat, he learned that unity was critical. He gathered others around him to seek God together as they went to unity in the Spirit in belief of the promise, and to confirm what God was speaking. Now more than ever, we must trust in God's promises and His wisdom instead of relying on our own human instincts or desires. He will give to us His wisdom and promises, and He will deliver us.

Word Meanings:
Keep: to attend to carefully, take care of
Unity: unanimity, agreement
Perfecting: complete furnishing, equipping
Edifying: building, building up
Unity: unanimity, agreement
Fullness: in the New Testament, the body of believers, as that which is filled with the presence, power, agency, riches of God, and of Christ

LESSON 6:
HOW DO WE OPERATE IN FAITH? (CONTINUED)

> - **James 2:17-24: Reminds us to be obedient to what we are hearing:**
>
> [17] So also faith by itself, if it does not have works, is dead.
>
> [18] But someone will say, "You have faith and I have works." Show me your faith apart from your works, and I will show you my faith by my works. 19 You believe that God is one; you do well. Even the demons believe—and shudder! [20] Do you want to be shown, you foolish person, that faith apart from works is useless? [21] Was not Abraham our father justified by works when he offered up his son Isaac on the altar? [22] You see that faith was active along with his works, and faith was completed by his works; [23] and the Scripture was fulfilled that says, "Abraham believed God, and it was counted to him as righteousness"—and he was called a friend of God. [24] You see that a person is justified by works and not by faith alone.

_____

_____

_____

_____

It is very clear: faith without following what God is saying is dead (has no power). So, we can say we believe, but if we act the opposite or do not follow God's instructions or do not wait for Him to fulfill what He says because we do not believe, then we are not being obedient to Him and to what we believe (because we are acting and doing the opposite). This is why it is so important to stay in process, keep asking Him to give us the faith to finish the process, and be obedient to what He is saying, to any instructions of the steps that He lays out (like Jehoshaphat did in the example above—he had to go to a specific location armed up for battle though God had said he was not going to have to fight the battle). Obedience will show our willingness to stay in process and take us to the places where God's will can be fulfilled—as He needs to get us to the right place, with the right people at the right time for His will to be done.

Word Meanings: **Dead:** destitute of force or power, inactive, inoperative

LESSON 6:
HOW DO WE OPERATE IN FAITH? (CONTINUED)

- **Corinthians 4:13: Speak what we are receiving, believing:**

  [13] Since we have the same spirit of faith according to what has been written, "I believed, and so I spoke," we also believe, and so we also speak…

_____
_____
_____
_____

Word Meanings: **Speak:** to use words in order to declare one's mind and disclose one's thoughts

- **Mark 11:20-25:**

  The Lesson from the Withered Fig Tree

  [20] As they passed by in the morning, they saw the fig tree withered away to its roots. [21] And Peter remembered and said to him, "Rabbi, look! The fig tree that you cursed has withered." [22] And Jesus answered them, "Have faith in God. [23] Truly, I say to you, whoever says to this mountain, 'Be taken up and thrown into the sea,' and does not doubt in his heart, but believes that what he says will come to pass, it will be done for him. [24] Therefore I tell you, whatever you ask in prayer, believe that you have received[a] it, and it will be yours. [25] And whenever you stand praying, forgive, if you have anything against anyone, so that your Father also who is in heaven may forgive you your trespasses."[b]

_____
_____
_____
_____

Word Meanings:
Doubt: waver, dispute about it
Believe: think to be true
Desire: same as ask
Receive: take to one's self, to own, to possess
Have: shall come about in reality

LESSON 6:
HOW DO WE OPERATE IN FAITH? (CONTINUED)

As you are moving to the "certainty" of faith, you are asked by God to speak publicly to others the Word that you have been given (spoken to you). This will illustrate to others the total certainty you have in your heart (faith) that God's promise will be kept. As you speak this, it actually cements it further into your heart. The key is that you do have clarity of what God spoke (and thus have taken the time to process that and have gone to unity with another to receive confirmation). God has given you faith because you stayed in process through your abiding (faith comes from hearing from the Word). You speak it; you speak to the mountain; you speak your authority in prayer—as you now move to Amen—so be it!

- **1 Timothy 4:6-11: Teach to others what you are learning as this builds faith:**

    A Good Servant of Christ Jesus
    6 If you put these things before the brothers,[a] you will be a good servant of Christ Jesus, being trained in the words of the faith and of the good doctrine that you have followed. 7 Have nothing to do with irreverent, silly myths. Rather train yourself for godliness; 8 for while bodily training is of some value, godliness is of value in every way, as it holds promise for the present life and also for the life to come. 9 The saying is trustworthy and deserving of full acceptance. 10 For to this end we toil and strive,[b] because we have our hope set on the living God, who is the Savior of all people, especially of those who believe.

    11 Command and teach these things.

_____
_____
_____
_____
_____

As you are learning this, God will ask you to share what you are learning, to teach others what you are learning. Think about how important this is: All believers must walk by faith for without faith it is impossible to please Him. This is not an intellectual truth, meaning something that is nice to know, but rather something that must be lived out. Otherwise, it is meaningless. So, God says for us to learn it, and then pass it along to others as it will multiply and serve the grand purpose, the bigger story of God. As you experience this, we believe that people will "line up around the block" to learn this as well, as they will see great and

LESSON 6:
HOW DO WE OPERATE IN FAITH? (CONTINUED)

mighty things happen in your life that they will want to know how to experience God's plan as well. When you share that you learned to walk by faith, others will want to know if they can learn that as well. Once they learn what you have, they can also begin to experience all that God has offered…and eventually they will be asked to share their knowledge and experience as well!

Word Meanings: **Command:** transmit a message along from one to another, to declare, announce
Teach: to hold discourse with others in order to instruct them, deliver didactic discourses

> - **Romans 1:17: Take it step by step, relax:**
>
> [17] For in it the righteousness of God is revealed from faith for faith,[a] as it is written, "The righteous shall live by faith."[b]

_____
_____
_____
_____
_____

As we live out this life of faith, the Father wants us to relax, to not feel any pressure about thinking we have to get it all right immediately or that we will be overwhelmed. Instead, stay in process and understand He will take us step by step, faith by faith. It will be a lifetime of situations, life challenges, etc. that He will be presenting, so we can never create a "safe, protected" life but we are to enjoy the life of walking step by step in faith.

WHAT ARE THE RESULTS OF FAITH?

Read through the following verses and write out the wonderful results of walking by faith. How should that change our life and strengthen our desire and heart for learning to walk by faith? Why?

> - **Mark 9:23: Will believe that nothing is impossible:**
>
> [23] And Jesus said to him, "'If you can'! All things are possible for one who believes."

LESSON 6:
HOW DO WE OPERATE IN FAITH? (CONTINUED)

_____
_____
_____
_____
_____

As we grow in faith, we will begin to personally see that all things are possible as nothing is impossible for God. He is the great "I Am" and no matter what the circumstances, the situation, or how dire things are, He can overcome and can provide a solution, a way through. The spiritual trumps the material, and He can make things happen. We will be the recipient of seeing this firsthand.

Word Meanings: **All Things:** each, every, any, all, the whole, everyone, everything
Possible: to be able (to do something), mighty, excelling in something, having power for something

> - **Romans 4:21: Will be persuaded that God will perform what He speaks:**
>
>   [21] fully convinced that God was able to do what he had promised.

_____
_____
_____
_____
_____

As we continue to walk by faith, we will be persuaded that what God speaks, He is fully able to perform. Our confidence will grow: our confidence in hearing, our confidence in Him giving us faith, our confidence in Him performing what He has spoken to us. He will use the ongoing process to persuade us. The key is not to shrink back or go back to figuring things out on our own. Keep being persuaded.

Word Meanings: **Be Persuaded:** persuaded, fully convinced or assured
Perform: to a promise

LESSON 6:
HOW DO WE OPERATE IN FAITH? (CONTINUED)

> - **Matthew 8:5-13:**
>
> The Faith of a Centurion
> [5] When he had entered Capernaum, a centurion came forward to him, appealing to him,[6] "Lord, my servant is lying paralyzed at home, suffering terribly." [7] And he said to him, "I will come and heal him." [8] But the centurion replied, "Lord, I am not worthy to have you come under my roof, but only say the word, and my servant will be healed. [9] For I too am a man under authority, with soldiers under me. And I say to one, 'Go,' and he goes, and to another, 'Come,' and he comes, and to my servant,[a] 'Do this,' and he does it." [10] When Jesus heard this, he marveled and said to those who followed him, "Truly, I tell you, with no one in Israel[b] have I found such faith. [11] I tell you, many will come from east and west and recline at table with Abraham, Isaac, and Jacob in the kingdom of heaven, [12] while the sons of the kingdom will be thrown into the outer darkness. In that place there will be weeping and gnashing of teeth." [13] And to the centurion Jesus said, "Go; let it be done for you as you have believed." And the servant was healed at that very moment.

_____
_____
_____
_____
_____

   As the centurion understood and as he was commended by Jesus for having such a great faith, we similarly will live out the process: receive a Word, believe the Word, and see it happen. We learn it firsthand and grow in it so that we stand on it as the centurion did. We expect it and process it all the time because we understand the authority and power of God and that it is personally applied to us in our individual circumstances. All of this is based upon the process of faith that we have learned.

Word Meanings: **Speak:** say
Word: logos
Healed: cure, to make whole
Marveled: wonder, wonder at

LESSON 6:
HOW DO WE OPERATE IN FAITH? (CONTINUED)

- **James 1:3: Will be tested:**

  3 for you know that the testing of your faith produces steadfastness.

_____
_____
_____
_____

We will expect to be tested. This is not to condemn us or show us "what is wrong with us," but rather as an assessment. Since He is the finisher of faith, He needs to show us if we are finished or not. A test will illustrate to us that yes, even though our current circumstances (a trial) are not going well, we can be certain that what God has spoken is true and is going to happen. We can be at peace and settled, or He will reveal our doubt, worry, and anxiety, which tend to cause us to develop our own plan B, C, etc. If we pass His tests, hallelujah, we stay settled and keep praying. Amen to this! But if we do not pass, we stay in process and understand that He has more work to do in us to finish. We must continue to abide so that we might reach the faith He has for us. Remember, it is His work, not ours, to work harder. We will be tested again until we pass.

Joy: gladness
Trials: experiment, attempt, proving
Testing: the proving

- **Mark 11:20-25: We will experience what God speaks:**

  The Lesson from the Withered Fig Tree
  20 As they passed by in the morning, they saw the fig tree withered away to its roots. 21 And Peter remembered and said to him, "Rabbi, look! The fig tree that you cursed has withered." 22 And Jesus answered them, "Have faith in God. 23 Truly, I say to you, whoever says to this mountain, 'Be taken up and thrown into the sea,' and does not doubt in his heart, but believes that what he says will come to pass, it will be done for him. 24 Therefore I tell you, whatever you ask in prayer, believe that you have received[a] it, and it will be yours. 25 And whenever you stand praying, forgive, if you have anything against anyone, so that your Father also who is in heaven may forgive you your trespasses."[b]

LESSON 6:
HOW DO WE OPERATE IN FAITH? (CONTINUED)

_____
_____
_____
_____
_____

One key to remember is that this process is not hypothetical (it has to translate into reality), and the promise(s) will be fulfilled as He spoke. If it never happens, then none of this is true—but it will happen. We will see God work. We will see God's Word come to pass. We will experience the fullness of joy from things actually happening. It will be thrilling, and we will bear witness to the glory of God. We will be able to tell the whole story, not just the end of what God said: He spoke to us (authored faith); we stayed in process, and He finished faith; it happened. All to the glory of God: We experienced His wonder, and our circumstance changed; we are persuaded; our confidence grew; and others will want to learn what we have learned.

Word Meanings: **Come to pass:** of miracles, to be performed, wrought
Have: will be, done already

> - **Ephesians 1:18-22: Will experience heavenly resurrection power in our everyday lives:**
>
> [18] having the eyes of your hearts enlightened, that you may know what is the hope to which he has called you, what are the riches of his glorious inheritance in the saints, [19] and what is the immeasurable greatness of his power toward us who believe, according to the working of his great might [20] that he worked in Christ when he raised him from the dead and seated him at his right hand in the heavenly places, [21] far above all rule and authority and power and dominion, and above every name that is named, not only in this age but also in the one to come. [22] And he put all things under his feet and gave him as head over all things to the church…

_____
_____
_____
_____
_____

LESSON 6:
HOW DO WE OPERATE IN FAITH? (CONTINUED)

Our prayer and our expectations are that His resurrection power will be directed toward those of us who believe. It will be spectacular, and it will be part of our lives—not once in a while and not just for a few—but for all of us who believe to experience regularly.

Word Meanings:
Exceeding: beyond anything
Greatness: of God's preeminent blessings
Power: power for performing miracles
Working: efficiency - in the New Testament used only of supernatural power

> - **1 John 5:4-5: Will overcome troubles and patterns of life and see real transformation of our soul:**
>
> ⁴ For everyone who has been born of God overcomes the world. And this is the victory that has overcome the world—our faith. ⁵ Who is it that overcomes the world except the one who believes that Jesus is the Son of God?

_____
_____
_____
_____
_____

As part of life, we will—or do—have troubles and tribulations, and we also have patterns within our souls that need healing (i.e., patterns of anger, worry, fear, frustration, addiction, unforgiveness, denial, etc.). As He leads us in faith, we will be "overcomers." We will see these troubles and tribulations overcome (conquered as we gain victory over them); and our patterns truly healed (not just managed but transformed so we no longer have the pattern to deal with but live in complete freedom). He will guide us and lead us into experiencing all of these step by step—a walk of faith as He directs so our lives will be victorious.

Word Meanings: **Overcome:** to conquer; to carry off the victory, come off victorious

LESSON 7:
WHAT ARE THE RESULTS OF FAITH? (CONTINUED)

As in Session 6, continue to read through the following verses and write out the wonderful results of walking by faith. How should that change our life and strengthen our desire or heart for learning to walk by faith? Why?

- **Mark 16:17-18; Hebrews 2:1-4: Will experience signs and wonders:**
  ¹⁷ And these signs will accompany those who believe: in my name they will cast out demons; they will speak in new tongues; ¹⁸ they will pick up serpents with their hands; and if they drink any deadly poison, it will not hurt them; they will lay their hands on the sick, and they will recover."

  Warning Against Neglecting Salvation
  2 Therefore we must pay much closer attention to what we have heard, lest we drift away from it. ² For since the message declared by angels proved to be reliable, and every transgression or disobedience received a just retribution, ³ how shall we escape if we neglect such a great salvation? It was declared at first by the Lord, and it was attested to us by those who heard, ⁴ while God also bore witness by signs and wonders and various miracles and by gifts of the Holy Spirit distributed according to his will.

"As we learn to walk by Faith, His will is for us to experience supernatural miracles, signs, and wonders."

_____
_____
_____
_____
_____

LESSON 7:
WHAT ARE THE RESULTS OF FAITH? (CONTINUED)

As we learn to walk by Faith, His will is for us to experience supernatural miracles, signs, and wonders. He tells us not to neglect so great a salvation by ignoring that God wishes to bear witness to the wonderful life He has planned for us through miracles, signs, and wonders, and gifts of the Holy Spirit. When we speak of Jesus, it will not be just a discussion about Him being our "ticket to heaven," but normal for us to share our experiences and demonstrate the wonderful supernatural things that only God can do as part of His will for us. He delivers these constantly as we continually walk by faith. It will happen all the time, and we will openly share that it was all God's doing (and not our own). How fantastic will that be!

Word Meanings: **Sign:** prodigy, portent, i.e., an unusual occurrence, transcending the common course of nature, of signs portending remarkable events soon to happen, of miracles and wonders by which God authenticates the men sent by Him, or by which men prove that the cause they are pleading is God's
Wonders: miracle performed by anyone
Miracles: power

- **Matthew 8:1-9: Will experience the Supernatural: (spend time reading through these stories and note the experiences of those who believed):**

Jesus Cleanses a Leper
8 When he came down from the mountain, great crowds followed him. ² And behold, a leper[a] came to him and knelt before him, saying, "Lord, if you will, you can make me clean."³ And Jesus[b] stretched out his hand and touched him, saying, "I will; be clean." And immediately his leprosy was cleansed. ⁴ And Jesus said to him, "See that you say nothing to anyone, but go, show yourself to the priest and offer the gift that Moses commanded, for a proof to them."

The Faith of a Centurion
⁵ When he had entered Capernaum, a centurion came forward to him, appealing to him,⁶ "Lord, my servant is lying paralyzed at home, suffering terribly." ⁷ And he said to him, "I will come and heal him." ⁸ But the centurion replied, "Lord, I am not worthy to have you come under my roof, but only say the word, and my servant will be healed. ⁹ For I too am a man under authority, with soldiers under me. And I say to one, 'Go,' and he goes, and to another, 'Come,' and he comes, and to my servant,[c] 'Do this,' and he does it."

LESSON 7:
WHAT ARE THE RESULTS OF FAITH? (CONTINUED)

_____
_____
_____
_____
_____

Note in these stories that both the role of faith (our willingness to hear what Jesus spoke and then believe what He spoke as He then performed what He spoke), and then see the willingness to follow Jesus as He was persuading His disciples of the power and authority that He has as He shows again how the spiritual overrules the material. He was demonstrating first-hand the process of faith, and the power of the spiritual over circumstances and the material. Let these stories build your faith and trust in the process.

Word Meanings: **Cleanse:** cure, heal
Heal: restore completely, make whole
Faith: great conviction, convinced
Cast Out: driven away, deprived of power
Word: logos
Healed: restore completely, make whole
All: each individually
Sick: miserable, ill
Infirmity: weakness, diseases
Sickness: disease

- **Romans 12:3-8: Will experience supernatural work of the Holy Spirit here amongst Christians:**

  Gifts of Grace
  [3] For by the grace given to me I say to everyone among you not to think of himself more highly than he ought to think, but to think with sober judgment, each according to the measure of faith that God has assigned. [4] For as in one body we have many members,[a] and the members do not all have the same function, [5] so we, though many, are one body in Christ, and individually members one of another. [6] Having gifts that differ according to the grace given to us, let us use them: if prophecy, in proportion to our

LESSON 7:
WHAT ARE THE RESULTS OF FAITH? (CONTINUED)

> faith; [7] if service, in our serving; the one who teaches, in his teaching; [8] the one who exhorts, in his exhortation; the one who contributes, in generosity; the one who leads,[b] with zeal; the one who does acts of mercy, with cheerfulness.

_____
_____
_____
_____
_____

In manifesting these gifts, the Spirit does so at a specific time to exercise a special manifestation for the sake of building up the body. This does not mean that certain people have these gifts permanently but that we all will have these gifts at certain times when so designated by the Spirit (and thus will be part of us joining His will). For example, some of these gifts are wisdom, which we have previously learned we are to all ask for and will receive; or faith, which we know we must have to please Him. This does not mean that certain believers are given these gifts and others are not. If that were the case, the other verses about wisdom or faith are not true and would put us in an impossible situation whereby we could not meet the condition set forth for living out the life of God. So, what this list here means is that these gifts are special manifestations given at specific times when God's gifting is needed for the body. We all can and will experience these as He so chooses. We just need to be open to these and realize that since He directs our lives with His will, we are to willingly be used with these gifts and look forward to these gifts being exercised for His purposes. Read through the definitions to understand what they mean.

Word Meanings:

Manifests: make actual and visible, realized, to make known by teaching to become manifest, be made known, of a person

Word: uttered by a living voice, embodies a conception or idea, what someone has said, the sayings of God

Wisdom: the act of interpreting dreams and always giving the sagest advice, the intelligence evinced in discovering the meaning of some mysterious number or vision, skill in the management of affairs, devout and proper prudence and discourse with men.

Knowledge: knowledge signifies general intelligence, understanding, to learn to know, come to know, get a knowledge of, perceive, feel

LESSON 7:
WHAT ARE THE RESULTS OF FAITH? (CONTINUED)

Faith: conviction of the truth of anything, belief; in the New Testament of a conviction or belief respecting man's relationship to God and divine things, generally with the included idea of trust and holy fervor born of faith and joined with it

Healing: to cure, heal, to make whole, to free from errors and sins, to bring about (one's) salvation

Miracles: strength power, ability, inherent power, power residing in a thing by virtue of its nature, or which a person or thing exerts and puts forth, power for performing miracles

Prophecy: a discourse emanating from divine inspiration and declaring the purposes of God, whether by reproving and admonishing the wicked, or comforting the afflicted, or revealing things hidden; especially by foretelling future events

Discernment: to separate, make a distinction, discriminate, to prefer, to learn by discrimination, to try, decide, to determine, give judgment, decide a dispute

Tongue: the language or dialect used by a particular people distinct from that of other nations

Interpretation: to translate what has been spoken or written in a foreign tongue into the vernacular

---

- **James 5:13-15: Will be a conduit and experience healing:**

    The Prayer of Faith
    [13] Is anyone among you suffering? Let him pray. Is anyone cheerful? Let him sing praise. [14] Is anyone among you sick? Let him call for the elders of the church, and let them pray over him, anointing him with oil in the name of the Lord. [15] And the prayer of faith will save the one who is sick, and the Lord will raise him up. And if he has committed sins, he will be forgiven.

_____
_____
_____
_____
_____

LESSON 7:
WHAT ARE THE RESULTS OF FAITH? (CONTINUED)

As we are learning how to walk in faith, others can and should call us (men and women of faith) to come into situations that need healing, supernatural work because of sickness, disease, problems, trouble, tribulation, etc. We cannot just pray and expect a solution per se because we are praying. We have learned faith and know this is not of us, and we cannot just decide on our own that we want something to happen. Instead, we first go to God and see what He has to say. Then, upon hearing Him author faith (He speaks), we ask Him to finish faith, and we can then pray over this situation and expect it to happen. We are always to ask for wisdom, because there might be sin in the camp, some other instruction that is needed, an unwillingness to cooperate, a reason that is blocking faith (see prior sessions), etc. Remember, this is not us claiming or taking charge—we are to go into process. And, since we know the process, we can be the ones that God uses to bring about His supernatural work and teach others what we have learned by leading the process. It is a wonderful way for God to be glorified and multiply the truth about living by faith.

Word Meanings: **Heal:** to save, keep safe and sound, to rescue from danger or destruction

> - **Acts 3:11-16: Will experience healing, wholeness:**
>
> Peter Speaks in Solomon's Portico
> [11] While he clung to Peter and John, all the people, utterly astounded, ran together to them in the portico called Solomon's. [12] And when Peter saw it he addressed the people: "Men of Israel, why do you wonder at this, or why do you stare at us, as though by our own power or piety we have made him walk? [13] The God of Abraham, the God of Isaac, and the God of Jacob, the God of our fathers, glorified his servant[a] Jesus, whom you delivered over and denied in the presence of Pilate, when he had decided to release him. [14] But you denied the Holy and Righteous One, and asked for a murderer to be granted to you, [15] and you killed the Author of life, whom God raised from the dead. To this we are witnesses. [16] And his name—by faith in his name—has made this man strong whom you see and know, and the faith that is through Jesus[b] has given the man this perfect health in the presence of you all.

_____
_____
_____
_____
_____

LESSON 7:
WHAT ARE THE RESULTS OF FAITH? (CONTINUED)

Word Meanings: **Name:** is used for everything which the name covers, everything the thought or feeling of which is aroused in the mind by mentioning, hearing, remembering the name, i.e. for one's rank, authority, interests, pleasure, command, excellences, deeds etc.
Soundness: of an unimpaired condition of the body, in which all its members are healthy and fit for use, wholeness

> - **Acts 14:9-18:**
>
> [9] He listened to Paul speaking. And Paul, looking intently at him and seeing that he had faith to be made well,[a] [10] said in a loud voice, "Stand upright on your feet." And he sprang up and began walking. [11] And when the crowds saw what Paul had done, they lifted up their voices, saying in Lycaonian, "The gods have come down to us in the likeness of men!" [12] Barnabas they called Zeus, and Paul, Hermes, because he was the chief speaker. [13] And the priest of Zeus, whose temple was at the entrance to the city, brought oxen and garlands to the gates and wanted to offer sacrifice with the crowds. [14] But when the apostles Barnabas and Paul heard of it, they tore their garments and rushed out into the crowd, crying out, [15] "Men, why are you doing these things? We also are men, of like nature with you, and we bring you good news, that you should turn from these vain things to a living God, who made the heaven and the earth and the sea and all that is in them. [16] In past generations he allowed all the nations to walk in their own ways. [17] Yet he did not leave himself without witness, for he did good by giving you rains from heaven and fruitful seasons, satisfying your hearts with food and gladness." [18] Even with these words they scarcely restrained the people from offering sacrifice to them.

_____
_____
_____
_____
_____

As we have stated, as we walk by faith, we will learn and have more and more clarity that God brings healing, wholeness, and completeness to our lives. It is not our doing, not our wishful thinking or prayers of hope, but the process of faith—hearing what He speaks, believing what He speaks and experiencing what He has spoken—all by faith in His name. He is the great "I Am" and nothing is impossible for Him. The spiritual trumps our circumstances.

LESSON 7:
WHAT ARE THE RESULTS OF FAITH? (CONTINUED)

Word Meanings: **Perceive:** notice, discern, discover

Healed: save, keep safe and sound, to rescue from danger or destruction

---

- **Acts 16:1-5: Will be strengthened in our soul, our purpose, our walk:**

Timothy Joins Paul and Silas

16 Paul[a] came also to Derbe and to Lystra. A disciple was there, named Timothy, the son of a Jewish woman who was a believer, but his father was a Greek. ² He was well spoken of by the brothers[b] at Lystra and Iconium. ³ Paul wanted Timothy to accompany him, and he took him and circumcised him because of the Jews who were in those places, for they all knew that his father was a Greek. ⁴ As they went on their way through the cities, they delivered to them for observance the decisions that had been reached by the apostles and elders who were in Jerusalem. ⁵ So the churches were strengthened in the faith, and they increased in numbers daily.

_____
_____
_____
_____
_____

This is the process:
1. We wonder if what He promises is true.
2. We consider whether it is true to our own thinking.
3. We recognize that the promises are absolutely true in the essence of my soul, my being.
4. We live it out in the purpose of our life and our walk with God.

My walk changes as I change: I go from "whatever happens, happens" thinking, to one who follows the process. My soul then is strengthened to the point of fully understanding, and I live it out as a way of life.

Word Meanings: **Established:** to make solid, make firm, strengthen, make strong

LESSON 7:
WHAT ARE THE RESULTS OF FAITH? (CONTINUED)

- **Ephesians 6:10-20: Will overcome the power of Satan – make him of no effect:**

The Whole Armor of God
[10] Finally, be strong in the Lord and in the strength of his might. [11] Put on the whole armor of God, that you may be able to stand against the schemes of the devil. [12] For we do not wrestle against flesh and blood, but against the rulers, against the authorities, against the cosmic powers over this present darkness, against the spiritual forces of evil in the heavenly places. [13] Therefore take up the whole armor of God, that you may be able to withstand in the evil day, and having done all, to stand firm. [14] Stand therefore, having fastened on the belt of truth, and having put on the breastplate of righteousness, [15] and, as shoes for your feet, having put on the readiness given by the gospel of peace. [16] In all circumstances take up the shield of faith, with which you can extinguish all the flaming darts of the evil one; [17] and take the helmet of salvation, and the sword of the Spirit, which is the word of God, [18] praying at all times in the Spirit, with all prayer and supplication. To that end, keep alert with all perseverance, making supplication for all the saints, [19] and also for me, that words may be given to me in opening my mouth boldly to proclaim the mystery of the gospel, [20] for which I am an ambassador in chains, that I may declare it boldly, as I ought to speak.

_____
_____
_____
_____
_____

Word Meanings:

Be Strong: endue with strength, strengthen
Power: force, strength
Might: mighty with great power; ability, force, strength
Stand: to uphold or sustain the authority or force of anything
Wiles: cunning arts, deceit, craft, trickery
Quench: to suppress, extinguish

LESSON 7:
WHAT ARE THE RESULTS OF FAITH? (CONTINUED)

> - **John 11:40-44: Will have our walk in life glorify God:**
>
> ⁴⁰ Jesus said to her, "Did I not tell you that if you believed you would see the glory of God?"⁴¹ So they took away the stone. And Jesus lifted up his eyes and said, "Father, I thank you that you have heard me. ⁴² I knew that you always hear me, but I said this on account of the people standing around, that they may believe that you sent me." ⁴³ When he had said these things, he cried out with a loud voice, "Lazarus, come out." ⁴⁴ The man who had died came out, his hands and feet bound with linen strips, and his face wrapped with a cloth. Jesus said to them, "Unbind him, and let him go."

_____
_____
_____
_____
_____

    As we have been seeing, our walk in faith is meant to glorify God. It is God's work from the beginning to the end of the process. He speaks to us His Word (authors the process). He finishes the process to certainty until we believe it. He then performs what He says (and what He performs is something that we cannot do on our own, because it is bigger and requires something that is not just natural), which by definition will bring glory to God. This is the very purpose of walking by faith. And we will easily bear witness to that.

Word Meanings: **Glory:** splendor, brightness, magnificence, excellence, preeminence, dignity, grace, majesty

LESSON 8:
EXAMPLES

Now that you have learned about the truths of living by faith, read through the following verses and write down what you observe about the keys to living by faith and how it works. What did God speak? How did they seek God? How did they stay with it through to belief? How did they experience God performing what He said? How then can you apply these truths to your life?

- **JOSHUA: 1:1-18; 5:13-15; 6:1-8:35:**

  God Commissions Joshua
  1 After the death of Moses the servant of the Lord, the Lord said to Joshua the son of Nun, Moses' assistant, ² "Moses my servant is dead. Now therefore arise, go over this Jordan, you and all this people, into the land that I am giving to them, to the people of Israel. ³ Every place that the sole of your foot will tread upon I have given to you, just as I promised to Moses. ⁴ From the wilderness and this Lebanon as far as the great river, the river Euphrates, all the land of the Hittites to the Great Sea toward the going down of the sun shall be your territory.⁵ No man shall be able to stand before you all the days of your life. Just as I was with Moses, so I will be with you. I will not leave you or forsake you. ⁶ Be strong and courageous, for you shall cause this people to inherit the land that I swore to their fathers to give them. ⁷ Only be strong and very courageous, being careful to do according to all the law that Moses my servant commanded you. Do not turn from it to the right hand or to the left, that you may have good success[a] wherever you go. ⁸ This Book of the Law shall not depart from your mouth, but you shall meditate on it day and night, so that you may be careful to do according to all that is written in it. For then you will make your way prosperous, and then you will have good success. ⁹ Have I not commanded you? Be strong and courageous. Do not be frightened, and do not be dismayed, for the Lord your God is with you wherever you go."

LESSON 8:
EXAMPLES

Joshua Assumes Command

10 And Joshua commanded the officers of the people, 11 "Pass through the midst of the camp and command the people, 'Prepare your provisions, for within three days you are to pass over this Jordan to go in to take possession of the land that the Lord your God is giving you to possess.'"

12 And to the Reubenites, the Gadites, and the half-tribe of Manasseh Joshua said, 13 "Remember the word that Moses the servant of the Lord commanded you, saying, 'The Lord your God is providing you a place of rest and will give you this land.' 14 Your wives, your little ones, and your livestock shall remain in the land that Moses gave you beyond the Jordan, but all the men of valor among you shall pass over armed before your brothers and shall help them, 15 until the Lord gives rest to your brothers as he has to you, and they also take possession of the land that the Lord your God is giving them. Then you shall return to the land of your possession and shall possess it, the land that Moses the servant of the Lord gave you beyond the Jordan toward the sunrise."

16 And they answered Joshua, "All that you have commanded us we will do, and wherever you send us we will go. 17 Just as we obeyed Moses in all things, so we will obey you. Only may the Lord your God be with you, as he was with Moses! 18 Whoever rebels against your commandment and disobeys your words, whatever you command him, shall be put to death. Only be strong and courageous."

The Commander of the Lord's Army

13 When Joshua was by Jericho, he lifted up his eyes and looked, and behold, a man was standing before him with his drawn sword in his hand. And Joshua went to him and said to him, "Are you for us, or for our adversaries?" 14 And he said, "No; but I am the commander of the army of the Lord. Now I have come." And Joshua fell on his face to the earth and worshiped[a] and said to him, "What does my lord say to his servant?" 15 And the commander of the Lord's army said to Joshua, "Take off your sandals from your feet, for the place where you are standing is holy." And Joshua did so.

The Fall of Jericho

6 Now Jericho was shut up inside and outside because of the people of Israel. None went out, and none came in. 2 And the Lord said to Joshua, "See, I have given Jericho into your hand, with its king and mighty men of valor. 3 You shall march around the city, all the men of war going around the city once. Thus shall

LESSON 8:
EXAMPLES

you do for six days. ⁴ Seven priests shall bear seven trumpets of rams' horns before the ark. On the seventh day you shall march around the city seven times, and the priests shall blow the trumpets. ⁵ And when they make a long blast with the ram's horn, when you hear the sound of the trumpet, then all the people shall shout with a great shout, and the wall of the city will fall down flat,[a] and the people shall go up, everyone straight before him." ⁶ So Joshua the son of Nun called the priests and said to them, "Take up the ark of the covenant and let seven priests bear seven trumpets of rams' horns before the ark of the Lord." ⁷ And he said to the people, "Go forward. March around the city and let the armed men pass on before the ark of the Lord."

⁸ And just as Joshua had commanded the people, the seven priests bearing the seven trumpets of rams' horns before the Lord went forward, blowing the trumpets, with the ark of the covenant of the Lord following them. ⁹ The armed men were walking before the priests who were blowing the trumpets, and the rear guard was walking after the ark, while the trumpets blew continually. ¹⁰ But Joshua commanded the people, "You shall not shout or make your voice heard, neither shall any word go out of your mouth, until the day I tell you to shout. Then you shall shout." ¹¹ So he caused the ark of the Lord to circle the city, going about it once. And they came into the camp and spent the night in the camp.

¹² Then Joshua rose early in the morning, and the priests took up the ark of the Lord. ¹³ And the seven priests bearing the seven trumpets of rams' horns before the ark of the Lord walked on, and they blew the trumpets continually. And the armed men were walking before them, and the rear guard was walking after the ark of the Lord, while the trumpets blew continually. ¹⁴ And the second day they marched around the city once, and returned into the camp. So they did for six days.

¹⁵ On the seventh day they rose early, at the dawn of day, and marched around the city in the same manner seven times. It was only on that day that they marched around the city seven times. ¹⁶ And at the seventh time, when the priests had blown the trumpets, Joshua said to the people, "Shout, for the Lord has given you the city. ¹⁷ And the city and all that is within it shall be devoted to the Lord for destruction.[b] Only Rahab the prostitute and all who are with her in her house shall live, because she hid the messengers whom we sent. ¹⁸ But you, keep yourselves from the things devoted to destruction, lest

LESSON 8:
EXAMPLES

when you have devoted them you take any of the devoted things and make the camp of Israel a thing for destruction and bring trouble upon it. [19] But all silver and gold, and every vessel of bronze and iron, are holy to the Lord; they shall go into the treasury of the Lord." [20] So the people shouted, and the trumpets were blown. As soon as the people heard the sound of the trumpet, the people shouted a great shout, and the wall fell down flat, so that the people went up into the city, every man straight before him, and they captured the city. [21] Then they devoted all in the city to destruction, both men and women, young and old, oxen, sheep, and donkeys, with the edge of the sword.

[22] But to the two men who had spied out the land, Joshua said, "Go into the prostitute's house and bring out from there the woman and all who belong to her, as you swore to her."[23] So the young men who had been spies went in and brought out Rahab and her father and mother and brothers and all who belonged to her. And they brought all her relatives and put them outside the camp of Israel. [24] And they burned the city with fire, and everything in it. Only the silver and gold, and the vessels of bronze and of iron, they put into the treasury of the house of the Lord. [25] But Rahab the prostitute and her father's household and all who belonged to her, Joshua saved alive. And she has lived in Israel to this day, because she hid the messengers whom Joshua sent to spy out Jericho.

[26] Joshua laid an oath on them at that time, saying, "Cursed before the Lord be the man who rises up and rebuilds this city, Jericho.

"At the cost of his firstborn shall he
   lay its foundation,
and at the cost of his youngest son
   shall he set up its gates."
[27] So the Lord was with Joshua, and his fame was in all the land.

Israel Defeated at Ai
7 But the people of Israel broke faith in regard to the devoted things, for Achan the son of Carmi, son of Zabdi, son of Zerah, of the tribe of Judah, took some of the devoted things. And the anger of the Lord burned against the people of Israel.

LESSON 8:
EXAMPLES

² Joshua sent men from Jericho to Ai, which is near Beth-aven, east of Bethel, and said to them, "Go up and spy out the land." And the men went up and spied out Ai. ³ And they returned to Joshua and said to him, "Do not have all the people go up, but let about two or three thousand men go up and attack Ai. Do not make the whole people toil up there, for they are few." ⁴ So about three thousand men went up there from the people. And they fled before the men of Ai, ⁵ and the men of Ai killed about thirty-six of their men and chased them before the gate as far as Shebarim and struck them at the descent. And the hearts of the people melted and became as water.

⁶ Then Joshua tore his clothes and fell to the earth on his face before the ark of the Lord until the evening, he and the elders of Israel. And they put dust on their heads. ⁷ And Joshua said, "Alas, O Lord God, why have you brought this people over the Jordan at all, to give us into the hands of the Amorites, to destroy us? Would that we had been content to dwell beyond the Jordan! ⁸ O Lord, what can I say, when Israel has turned their backs before their enemies!⁹ For the Canaanites and all the inhabitants of the land will hear of it and will surround us and cut off our name from the earth. And what will you do for your great name?"

The Sin of Achan
¹⁰ The Lord said to Joshua, "Get up! Why have you fallen on your face? ¹¹ Israel has sinned; they have transgressed my covenant that I commanded them; they have taken some of the devoted things; they have stolen and lied and put them among their own belongings.¹² Therefore the people of Israel cannot stand before their enemies. They turn their backs before their enemies, because they have become devoted for destruction.[c] I will be with you no more, unless you destroy the devoted things from among you. ¹³ Get up! Consecrate the people and say, 'Consecrate yourselves for tomorrow; for thus says the Lord, God of Israel, "There are devoted things in your midst, O Israel. You cannot stand before your enemies until you take away the devoted things from among you." ¹⁴ In the morning therefore you shall be brought near by your tribes. And the tribe that the Lord takes by lot shall come near by clans. And the clan that the Lord takes shall come near by households. And the household that the Lord takes shall come near man by man. ¹⁵ And he who is taken with the devoted things shall be burned with fire, he and all that he has, because he has transgressed the covenant of the Lord, and because he has done an outrageous thing in Israel.'"

LESSON 8:
EXAMPLES

¹⁶ So Joshua rose early in the morning and brought Israel near tribe by tribe, and the tribe of Judah was taken. ¹⁷ And he brought near the clans of Judah, and the clan of the Zerahites was taken. And he brought near the clan of the Zerahites man by man, and Zabdi was taken. ¹⁸ And he brought near his household man by man, and Achan the son of Carmi, son of Zabdi, son of Zerah, of the tribe of Judah, was taken. ¹⁹ Then Joshua said to Achan, "My son, give glory to the Lord God of Israel and give praise[d] to him. And tell me now what you have done; do not hide it from me." ²⁰ And Achan answered Joshua, "Truly I have sinned against the Lord God of Israel, and this is what I did: ²¹ when I saw among the spoil a beautiful cloak from Shinar, and 200 shekels of silver, and a bar of gold weighing 50 shekels,[e] then I coveted them and took them. And see, they are hidden in the earth inside my tent, with the silver underneath."

²² So Joshua sent messengers, and they ran to the tent; and behold, it was hidden in his tent with the silver underneath. ²³ And they took them out of the tent and brought them to Joshua and to all the people of Israel. And they laid them down before the Lord. ²⁴ And Joshua and all Israel with him took Achan the son of Zerah, and the silver and the cloak and the bar of gold, and his sons and daughters and his oxen and donkeys and sheep and his tent and all that he had. And they brought them up to the Valley of Achor. ²⁵ And Joshua said, "Why did you bring trouble on us? The Lord brings trouble on you today." And all Israel stoned him with stones. They burned them with fire and stoned them with stones. ²⁶ And they raised over him a great heap of stones that remains to this day. Then the Lord turned from his burning anger. Therefore, to this day the name of that place is called the Valley of Achor.[f]

The Fall of Ai
8 And the Lord said to Joshua, "Do not fear and do not be dismayed. Take all the fighting men with you, and arise, go up to Ai. See, I have given into your hand the king of Ai, and his people, his city, and his land. ² And you shall do to Ai and its king as you did to Jericho and its king. Only its spoil and its livestock you shall take as plunder for yourselves. Lay an ambush against the city, behind it." ³ So Joshua and all the fighting men arose to go up to Ai. And Joshua chose 30,000 mighty men of valor and sent them out by night. ⁴ And he commanded them, "Behold, you shall lie in ambush against the city, behind it. Do not go very far from the city, but all of you remain ready. ⁵ And I and all the people who are with me will approach the city. And when they come out against us just

LESSON 8:
EXAMPLES

as before, we shall flee before them. ⁶ And they will come out after us, until we have drawn them away from the city. For they will say, 'They are fleeing from us, just as before.' So we will flee before them. ⁷ Then you shall rise up from the ambush and seize the city, for the Lord your God will give it into your hand. ⁸ And as soon as you have taken the city, you shall set the city on fire. You shall do according to the word of the Lord. See, I have commanded you." ⁹ So Joshua sent them out. And they went to the place of ambush and lay between Bethel and Ai, to the west of Ai, but Joshua spent that night among the people.

¹⁰ Joshua arose early in the morning and mustered the people and went up, he and the elders of Israel, before the people to Ai. ¹¹ And all the fighting men who were with him went up and drew near before the city and encamped on the north side of Ai, with a ravine between them and Ai. ¹² He took about 5,000 men and set them in ambush between Bethel and Ai, to the west of the city. ¹³ So they stationed the forces, the main encampment that was north of the city and its rear guard west of the city. But Joshua spent that night in the valley. ¹⁴ And as soon as the king of Ai saw this, he and all his people, the men of the city, hurried and went out early to the appointed place[g] toward the Arabah to meet Israel in battle. But he did not know that there was an ambush against him behind the city. ¹⁵ And Joshua and all Israel pretended to be beaten before them and fled in the direction of the wilderness. ¹⁶ So all the people who were in the city were called together to pursue them, and as they pursued Joshua they were drawn away from the city. ¹⁷ Not a man was left in Ai or Bethel who did not go out after Israel. They left the city open and pursued Israel.

¹⁸ Then the Lord said to Joshua, "Stretch out the javelin that is in your hand toward Ai, for I will give it into your hand." And Joshua stretched out the javelin that was in his hand toward the city. ¹⁹ And the men in the ambush rose quickly out of their place, and as soon as he had stretched out his hand, they ran and entered the city and captured it. And they hurried to set the city on fire. ²⁰ So when the men of Ai looked back, behold, the smoke of the city went up to heaven, and they had no power to flee this way or that, for the people who fled to the wilderness turned back against the pursuers. ²¹ And when Joshua and all Israel saw that the ambush had captured the city, and that the smoke of the city went up, then they turned back and struck down the men of Ai. ²² And the others came out from the city against them, so they were in the midst of Israel, some on this side, and some on that side. And Israel struck them down, until there was left none that survived or escaped. ²³ But the king of Ai they took alive, and brought him near to Joshua.

LESSON 8:
EXAMPLES

²⁴ When Israel had finished killing all the inhabitants of Ai in the open wilderness where they pursued them, and all of them to the very last had fallen by the edge of the sword, all Israel returned to Ai and struck it down with the edge of the sword. ²⁵ And all who fell that day, both men and women, were 12,000, all the people of Ai. ²⁶ But Joshua did not draw back his hand with which he stretched out the javelin until he had devoted all the inhabitants of Ai to destruction.[h] ²⁷ Only the livestock and the spoil of that city Israel took as their plunder, according to the word of the Lord that he commanded Joshua. ²⁸ So Joshua burned Ai and made it forever a heap of ruins, as it is to this day. ²⁹ And he hanged the king of Ai on a tree until evening. And at sunset Joshua commanded, and they took his body down from the tree and threw it at the entrance of the gate of the city and raised over it a great heap of stones, which stands there to this day.

Joshua Renews the Covenant
³⁰ At that time Joshua built an altar to the Lord, the God of Israel, on Mount Ebal, ³¹ just as Moses the servant of the Lord had commanded the people of Israel, as it is written in the Book of the Law of Moses, "an altar of uncut stones, upon which no man has wielded an iron tool." And they offered on it burnt offerings to the Lord and sacrificed peace offerings. ³² And there, in the presence of the people of Israel, he wrote on the stones a copy of the law of Moses, which he had written. ³³ And all Israel, sojourner as well as native born, with their elders and officers and their judges, stood on opposite sides of the ark before the Levitical priests who carried the ark of the covenant of the Lord, half of them in front of Mount Gerizim and half of them in front of Mount Ebal, just as Moses the servant of the Lord had commanded at the first, to bless the people of Israel. ³⁴ And afterward he read all the words of the law, the blessing and the curse, according to all that is written in the Book of the Law.³⁵ There was not a word of all that Moses commanded that Joshua did not read before all the assembly of Israel, and the women, and the little ones, and the sojourners who lived[i] among them.

_____
_____
_____
_____
_____

LESSON 8:
EXAMPLES

- **ABIJAH: 2 Chronicles 13:1-22:**

Abijah Reigns in Judah
13 In the eighteenth year of King Jeroboam, Abijah began to reign over Judah. ² He reigned for three years in Jerusalem. His mother's name was Micaiah[a] the daughter of Uriel of Gibeah.

Now there was war between Abijah and Jeroboam. ³ Abijah went out to battle, having an army of valiant men of war, 400,000 chosen men. And Jeroboam drew up his line of battle against him with 800,000 chosen mighty warriors. ⁴ Then Abijah stood up on Mount Zemaraim that is in the hill country of Ephraim and said, "Hear me, O Jeroboam and all Israel!⁵ Ought you not to know that the Lord God of Israel gave the kingship over Israel forever to David and his sons by a covenant of salt? ⁶ Yet Jeroboam the son of Nebat, a servant of Solomon the son of David, rose up and rebelled against his lord, ⁷ and certain worthless scoundrels[b] gathered about him and defied Rehoboam the son of Solomon, when Rehoboam was young and irresolute[c] and could not withstand them.

⁸ "And now you think to withstand the kingdom of the Lord in the hand of the sons of David, because you are a great multitude and have with you the golden calves that Jeroboam made you for gods. ⁹ Have you not driven out the priests of the Lord, the sons of Aaron, and the Levites, and made priests for yourselves like the peoples of other lands? Whoever comes for ordination[d] with a young bull or seven rams becomes a priest of what are not gods. ¹⁰ But as for us, the Lord is our God, and we have not forsaken him. We have priests ministering to the Lord who are sons of Aaron, and Levites for their service. ¹¹ They offer to the Lord every morning and every evening burnt offerings and incense of sweet spices, set out the showbread on the table of pure gold, and care for the golden lampstand that its lamps may burn every evening. For we keep the charge of the Lord our God, but you have forsaken him.¹² Behold, God is with us at our head, and his priests with their battle trumpets to sound the call to battle against you. O sons of Israel, do not fight against the Lord, the God of your fathers, for you cannot succeed."

¹³ Jeroboam had sent an ambush around to come upon them from behind. Thus his troops[e] were in front of Judah, and the ambush was behind them. ¹⁴ And when Judah looked, behold, the battle was in front of and behind them. And they cried to the Lord, and the priests blew the trumpets. ¹⁵ Then the men

LESSON 8:
EXAMPLES

of Judah raised the battle shout. And when the men of Judah shouted, God defeated Jeroboam and all Israel before Abijah and Judah. [16] The men of Israel fled before Judah, and God gave them into their hand. [17] Abijah and his people struck them with great force, so there fell slain of Israel 500,000 chosen men. [18] Thus the men of Israel were subdued at that time, and the men of Judah prevailed, because they relied on the Lord, the God of their fathers. [19] And Abijah pursued Jeroboam and took cities from him, Bethel with its villages and Jeshanah with its villages and Ephron[f] with its villages. [20] Jeroboam did not recover his power in the days of Abijah. And the Lord struck him down, and he died. [21] But Abijah grew mighty. And he took fourteen wives and had twenty-two sons and sixteen daughters. [22] The rest of the acts of Abijah, his ways and his sayings, are written in the story of the prophet Iddo.

_____
_____
_____
_____
_____
_____
_____
_____

- **JEHOSHAPHAT: 2 Chronicles 20:1-30:**

Jehoshaphat's Prayer
20 After this the Moabites and Ammonites, and with them some of the Meunites,[a] came against Jehoshaphat for battle. [2] Some men came and told Jehoshaphat, "A great multitude is coming against you from Edom,[b] from beyond the sea; and, behold, they are in Hazazon-tamar" (that is, Engedi). [3] Then Jehoshaphat was afraid and set his face to seek the Lord, and proclaimed a fast throughout all Judah. [4] And Judah assembled to seek help from the Lord; from all the cities of Judah they came to seek the Lord.

LESSON 8:
EXAMPLES

⁵ And Jehoshaphat stood in the assembly of Judah and Jerusalem, in the house of the Lord, before the new court, ⁶ and said, "O Lord, God of our fathers, are you not God in heaven? You rule over all the kingdoms of the nations. In your hand are power and might, so that none is able to withstand you. ⁷ Did you not, our God, drive out the inhabitants of this land before your people Israel, and give it forever to the descendants of Abraham your friend? ⁸ And they have lived in it and have built for you in it a sanctuary for your name, saying, ⁹ 'If disaster comes upon us, the sword, judgment,[c] or pestilence, or famine, we will stand before this house and before you—for your name is in this house—and cry out to you in our affliction, and you will hear and save.' ¹⁰ And now behold, the men of Ammon and Moab and Mount Seir, whom you would not let Israel invade when they came from the land of Egypt, and whom they avoided and did not destroy— ¹¹ behold, they reward us by coming to drive us out of your possession, which you have given us to inherit. ¹² O our God, will you not execute judgment on them? For we are powerless against this great horde that is coming against us. We do not know what to do, but our eyes are on you."

¹³ Meanwhile all Judah stood before the Lord, with their little ones, their wives, and their children. ¹⁴ And the Spirit of the Lord came[d] upon Jahaziel the son of Zechariah, son of Benaiah, son of Jeiel, son of Mattaniah, a Levite of the sons of Asaph, in the midst of the assembly. ¹⁵ And he said, "Listen, all Judah and inhabitants of Jerusalem and King Jehoshaphat: Thus says the Lord to you, 'Do not be afraid and do not be dismayed at this great horde, for the battle is not yours but God's. ¹⁶ Tomorrow go down against them. Behold, they will come up by the ascent of Ziz. You will find them at the end of the valley, east of the wilderness of Jeruel. ¹⁷ You will not need to fight in this battle. Stand firm, hold your position, and see the salvation of the Lord on your behalf, O Judah and Jerusalem.' Do not be afraid and do not be dismayed. Tomorrow go out against them, and the Lord will be with you."

¹⁸ Then Jehoshaphat bowed his head with his face to the ground, and all Judah and the inhabitants of Jerusalem fell down before the Lord, worshiping the Lord. ¹⁹ And the Levites, of the Kohathites and the Korahites, stood up to praise the Lord, the God of Israel, with a very loud voice.

²⁰ And they rose early in the morning and went out into the wilderness of Tekoa. And when they went out, Jehoshaphat stood and said, "Hear me, Judah and inhabitants of Jerusalem! Believe in the Lord your God, and you will be

LESSON 8:
EXAMPLES

established; believe his prophets, and you will succeed." 21 And when he had taken counsel with the people, he appointed those who were to sing to the Lord and praise him in holy attire, as they went before the army, and say,

"Give thanks to the Lord,
    for his steadfast love endures forever."

22 And when they began to sing and praise, the Lord set an ambush against the men of Ammon, Moab, and Mount Seir, who had come against Judah, so that they were routed. 23 For the men of Ammon and Moab rose against the inhabitants of Mount Seir, devoting them to destruction, and when they had made an end of the inhabitants of Seir, they all helped to destroy one another.

The Lord Delivers Judah
24 When Judah came to the watchtower of the wilderness, they looked toward the horde, and behold, there[e] were dead bodies lying on the ground; none had escaped. 25 When Jehoshaphat and his people came to take their spoil, they found among them, in great numbers, goods, clothing, and precious things, which they took for themselves until they could carry no more. They were three days in taking the spoil, it was so much. 26 On the fourth day they assembled in the Valley of Beracah,[f] for there they blessed the Lord. Therefore the name of that place has been called the Valley of Beracah to this day. 27 Then they returned, every man of Judah and Jerusalem, and Jehoshaphat at their head, returning to Jerusalem with joy, for the Lord had made them rejoice over their enemies. 28 They came to Jerusalem with harps and lyres and trumpets, to the house of the Lord. 29 And the fear of God came on all the kingdoms of the countries when they heard that the Lord had fought against the enemies of Israel. 30 So the realm of Jehoshaphat was quiet, for his God gave him rest all around.

LESSON 8:
EXAMPLES

- **PETER: Acts 3:1-16; 4:1-31; 5:1-32; 10:1-48:**

The Lame Beggar Healed
3 Now Peter and John were going up to the temple at the hour of prayer, the ninth hour.[a] 2 And a man lame from birth was being carried, whom they laid daily at the gate of the temple that is called the Beautiful Gate to ask alms of those entering the temple. 3 Seeing Peter and John about to go into the temple, he asked to receive alms. 4 And Peter directed his gaze at him, as did John, and said, "Look at us." 5 And he fixed his attention on them, expecting to receive something from them. 6 But Peter said, "I have no silver and gold, but what I do have I give to you. In the name of Jesus Christ of Nazareth, rise up and walk!" 7 And he took him by the right hand and raised him up, and immediately his feet and ankles were made strong. 8 And leaping up, he stood and began to walk, and entered the temple with them, walking and leaping and praising God. 9 And all the people saw him walking and praising God, 10 and recognized him as the one who sat at the Beautiful Gate of the temple, asking for alms. And they were filled with wonder and amazement at what had happened to him.

Peter Speaks in Solomon's Portico
11 While he clung to Peter and John, all the people, utterly astounded, ran together to them in the portico called Solomon's. 12 And when Peter saw it he addressed the people: "Men of Israel, why do you wonder at this, or why do you stare at us, as though by our own power or piety we have made him walk? 13 The God of Abraham, the God of Isaac, and the God of Jacob, the God of our fathers, glorified his servant[b] Jesus, whom you delivered over and denied in the presence of Pilate, when he had decided to release him. 14 But you denied the Holy and Righteous One, and asked for a murderer to be granted to you, 15 and you killed the Author of life, whom God raised from the dead. To this we are witnesses. 16 And his name—by faith in his name—has made this man strong whom you see and know, and the faith that is through Jesus[c] has given the man this perfect health in the presence of you all.

Peter and John Before the Council
4 And as they were speaking to the people, the priests and the captain of the temple and the Sadducees came upon them, 2 greatly annoyed because they were teaching the people and proclaiming in Jesus the resurrection from the dead. 3 And they arrested them and put them in custody until the next day, for it was already evening. 4 But many of those who had heard the word believed, and the number of the men came to about five thousand.

LESSON 8:
EXAMPLES

5 On the next day their rulers and elders and scribes gathered together in Jerusalem, 6 with Annas the high priest and Caiaphas and John and Alexander, and all who were of the high-priestly family. 7 And when they had set them in the midst, they inquired, "By what power or by what name did you do this?" 8 Then Peter, filled with the Holy Spirit, said to them, "Rulers of the people and elders, 9 if we are being examined today concerning a good deed done to a crippled man, by what means this man has been healed, 10 let it be known to all of you and to all the people of Israel that by the name of Jesus Christ of Nazareth, whom you crucified, whom God raised from the dead—by him this man is standing before you well. 11 This Jesus[a] is the stone that was rejected by you, the builders, which has become the cornerstone.[b] 12 And there is salvation in no one else, for there is no other name under heaven given among men[c] by which we must be saved."

13 Now when they saw the boldness of Peter and John, and perceived that they were uneducated, common men, they were astonished. And they recognized that they had been with Jesus. 14 But seeing the man who was healed standing beside them, they had nothing to say in opposition. 15 But when they had commanded them to leave the council, they conferred with one another, 16 saying, "What shall we do with these men? For that a notable sign has been performed through them is evident to all the inhabitants of Jerusalem, and we cannot deny it. 17 But in order that it may spread no further among the people, let us warn them to speak no more to anyone in this name." 18 So they called them and charged them not to speak or teach at all in the name of Jesus. 19 But Peter and John answered them, "Whether it is right in the sight of God to listen to you rather than to God, you must judge, 20 for we cannot but speak of what we have seen and heard." 21 And when they had further threatened them, they let them go, finding no way to punish them, because of the people, for all were praising God for what had happened. 22 For the man on whom this sign of healing was performed was more than forty years old.

The Believers Pray for Boldness
23 When they were released, they went to their friends and reported what the chief priests and the elders had said to them. 24 And when they heard it, they lifted their voices together to God and said, "Sovereign Lord, who made the heaven and the earth and the sea and everything in them, 25 who through the mouth of our father David, your servant,[d] said by the Holy Spirit,

LESSON 8:
EXAMPLES

> "'Why did the Gentiles rage,
>   and the peoples plot in vain?
> ²⁶ The kings of the earth set themselves,
>   and the rulers were gathered together,
>   against the Lord and against his Anointed'[e]—
>
> ²⁷ for truly in this city there were gathered together against your holy servant Jesus, whom you anointed, both Herod and Pontius Pilate, along with the Gentiles and the peoples of Israel, ²⁸ to do whatever your hand and your plan had predestined to take place. ²⁹ And now, Lord, look upon their threats and grant to your servants to continue to speak your word with all boldness, ³⁰ while you stretch out your hand to heal, and signs and wonders are performed through the name of your holy servant Jesus." ³¹ And when they had prayed, the place in which they were gathered together was shaken, and they were all filled with the Holy Spirit and continued to speak the word of God with boldness.
>
> Ananias and Sapphira
>
> **5** But a man named Ananias, with his wife Sapphira, sold a piece of property, ² and with his wife's knowledge he kept back for himself some of the proceeds and brought only a part of it and laid it at the apostles' feet. ³ But Peter said, "Ananias, why has Satan filled your heart to lie to the Holy Spirit and to keep back for yourself part of the proceeds of the land? ⁴ While it remained unsold, did it not remain your own? And after it was sold, was it not at your disposal? Why is it that you have contrived this deed in your heart? You have not lied to man but to God." ⁵ When Ananias heard these words, he fell down and breathed his last. And great fear came upon all who heard of it. ⁶ The young men rose and wrapped him up and carried him out and buried him.
>
> ⁷ After an interval of about three hours his wife came in, not knowing what had happened. ⁸ And Peter said to her, "Tell me whether you[a] sold the land for so much." And she said, "Yes, for so much." ⁹ But Peter said to her, "How is it that you have agreed together to test the Spirit of the Lord? Behold, the feet of those who have buried your husband are at the door, and they will carry you out." ¹⁰ Immediately she fell down at his feet and breathed her last. When the young men came in they found her dead, and they carried her out and buried her beside her husband. ¹¹ And great fear came upon the whole church and upon all who heard of these things.

LESSON 8:
EXAMPLES

Many Signs and Wonders Done

12 Now many signs and wonders were regularly done among the people by the hands of the apostles. And they were all together in Solomon's Portico. 13 None of the rest dared join them, but the people held them in high esteem. 14 And more than ever believers were added to the Lord, multitudes of both men and women, 15 so that they even carried out the sick into the streets and laid them on cots and mats, that as Peter came by at least his shadow might fall on some of them. 16 The people also gathered from the towns around Jerusalem, bringing the sick and those afflicted with unclean spirits, and they were all healed.

The Apostles Arrested and Freed

17 But the high priest rose up, and all who were with him (that is, the party of the Sadducees), and filled with jealousy 18 they arrested the apostles and put them in the public prison. 19 But during the night an angel of the Lord opened the prison doors and brought them out, and said, 20 "Go and stand in the temple and speak to the people all the words of this Life." 21 And when they heard this, they entered the temple at daybreak and began to teach.

Now when the high priest came, and those who were with him, they called together the council, all the senate of the people of Israel, and sent to the prison to have them brought. 22 But when the officers came, they did not find them in the prison, so they returned and reported, 23 "We found the prison securely locked and the guards standing at the doors, but when we opened them we found no one inside." 24 Now when the captain of the temple and the chief priests heard these words, they were greatly perplexed about them, wondering what this would come to. 25 And someone came and told them, "Look! The men whom you put in prison are standing in the temple and teaching the people." 26 Then the captain with the officers went and brought them, but not by force, for they were afraid of being stoned by the people.

27 And when they had brought them, they set them before the council. And the high priest questioned them, 28 saying, "We strictly charged you not to teach in this name, yet here you have filled Jerusalem with your teaching, and you intend to bring this man's blood upon us." 29 But Peter and the apostles answered, "We must obey God rather than men. 30 The God of our fathers raised Jesus, whom you killed by hanging him on a tree. 31 God exalted him at his right hand as Leader and Savior, to give repentance to Israel and forgiveness of sins. 32 And we are witnesses to these things, and so is the Holy Spirit, whom God has given to those who obey him."

LESSON 8:
EXAMPLES

Peter and Cornelius

10 At Caesarea there was a man named Cornelius, a centurion of what was known as the Italian Cohort, ² a devout man who feared God with all his household, gave alms generously to the people, and prayed continually to God. ³ About the ninth hour of the day[a] he saw clearly in a vision an angel of God come in and say to him, "Cornelius." ⁴ And he stared at him in terror and said, "What is it, Lord?" And he said to him, "Your prayers and your alms have ascended as a memorial before God. ⁵ And now send men to Joppa and bring one Simon who is called Peter. ⁶ He is lodging with one Simon, a tanner, whose house is by the sea." ⁷ When the angel who spoke to him had departed, he called two of his servants and a devout soldier from among those who attended him, 8 and having related everything to them, he sent them to Joppa.

Peter's Vision

⁹ The next day, as they were on their journey and approaching the city, Peter went up on the housetop about the sixth hour[b] to pray. ¹⁰ And he became hungry and wanted something to eat, but while they were preparing it, he fell into a trance ¹¹ and saw the heavens opened and something like a great sheet descending, being let down by its four corners upon the earth. ¹² In it were all kinds of animals and reptiles and birds of the air. ¹³ And there came a voice to him: "Rise, Peter; kill and eat." ¹⁴ But Peter said, "By no means, Lord; for I have never eaten anything that is common or unclean." ¹⁵ And the voice came to him again a second time, "What God has made clean, do not call common." ¹⁶ This happened three times, and the thing was taken up at once to heaven.

¹⁷ Now while Peter was inwardly perplexed as to what the vision that he had seen might mean, behold, the men who were sent by Cornelius, having made inquiry for Simon's house, stood at the gate ¹⁸ and called out to ask whether Simon who was called Peter was lodging there. ¹⁹ And while Peter was pondering the vision, the Spirit said to him, "Behold, three men are looking for you. ²⁰ Rise and go down and accompany them without hesitation,[c] for I have sent them." ²¹ And Peter went down to the men and said, "I am the one you are looking for. What is the reason for your coming?" ²² And they said, "Cornelius, a centurion, an upright and God-fearing man, who is well spoken of by the whole Jewish nation, was directed by a holy angel to send for you to come to his house and to hear what you have to say." ²³ So he invited them in to be his guests.

LESSON 8:
EXAMPLES

The next day he rose and went away with them, and some of the brothers from Joppa accompanied him. 24 And on the following day they entered Caesarea. Cornelius was expecting them and had called together his relatives and close friends. 25 When Peter entered, Cornelius met him and fell down at his feet and worshiped him. 26 But Peter lifted him up, saying, "Stand up; I too am a man." 27 And as he talked with him, he went in and found many persons gathered. 28 And he said to them, "You yourselves know how unlawful it is for a Jew to associate with or to visit anyone of another nation, but God has shown me that I should not call any person common or unclean. 29 So when I was sent for, I came without objection. I ask then why you sent for me."

30 And Cornelius said, "Four days ago, about this hour, I was praying in my house at the ninth hour,[d] and behold, a man stood before me in bright clothing 31 and said, 'Cornelius, your prayer has been heard and your alms have been remembered before God. 32 Send therefore to Joppa and ask for Simon who is called Peter. He is lodging in the house of Simon, a tanner, by the sea.' 33 So I sent for you at once, and you have been kind enough to come. Now therefore we are all here in the presence of God to hear all that you have been commanded by the Lord."

Gentiles Hear the Good News
34 So Peter opened his mouth and said: "Truly I understand that God shows no partiality, 35 but in every nation anyone who fears him and does what is right is acceptable to him. 36 As for the word that he sent to Israel, preaching good news of peace through Jesus Christ (he is Lord of all), 37 you yourselves know what happened throughout all Judea, beginning from Galilee after the baptism that John proclaimed: 38 how God anointed Jesus of Nazareth with the Holy Spirit and with power. He went about doing good and healing all who were oppressed by the devil, for God was with him. 39 And we are witnesses of all that he did both in the country of the Jews and in Jerusalem. They put him to death by hanging him on a tree, 40 but God raised him on the third day and made him to appear, 41 not to all the people but to us who had been chosen by God as witnesses, who ate and drank with him after he rose from the dead. 42 And he commanded us to preach to the people and to testify that he is the one appointed by God to be judge of the living and the dead. 43 To him all the prophets bear witness that everyone who believes in him receives forgiveness of sins through his name."

LESSON 8:
EXAMPLES

> **The Holy Spirit Falls on the Gentiles**
> ⁴⁴ While Peter was still saying these things, the Holy Spirit fell on all who heard the word. ⁴⁵ And the believers from among the circumcised who had come with Peter were amazed, because the gift of the Holy Spirit was poured out even on the Gentiles. ⁴⁶ For they were hearing them speaking in tongues and extolling God. Then Peter declared, ⁴⁷ "Can anyone withhold water for baptizing these people, who have received the Holy Spirit just as we have?" ⁴⁸ And he commanded them to be baptized in the name of Jesus Christ. Then they asked him to remain for some days.

www.ingramcontent.com/pod-product-compliance
Lightning Source LLC
Chambersburg PA
CBHW042026100526
44587CB00029B/4311